Lesson Planning Guides

Language
Network

McDougal Littell
A HOUGHTON MIFFLIN COMPANY

Evanston, Illinois • Boston • Dallas

Contents

Essential Writing Skills

32 **Preparing for Tests**

Special Features

This book provides a separate lesson plan for every lesson and Writing Workshop in the Pupil's Edition. By looking at each lesson plan, you can see a complete list of the teaching resources available for that lesson.

Each page clearly refers to its corresponding part in the Pupil's Edition for easy reference.

Teacher _____ Class _____ Date _____

Lesson 3

Using Verb Tenses

Lesson objectives

Pages 137–141

Lesson Plans correspond to lessons in the Pupil's Edition.

Lesson 3 Objectives
To recognize verb tenses and to use them in writing

THE LANGUAGE OF **LITERATURE** Connect to *Into Thin Air*, Level 9.

Connections to The Language of Literature are supplied for easy reference whenever possible.

Teach	Resources
Warm-Up ___ Test Preparation	☐ 📖 Daily Test Prep. p. DT17
Using the Pupil's Edition ___ Here's the Idea ___ Why It Matters in Writing	☐ Pupil's Edition p. 137 ☐ Pupil's Edition p. 140

Practice and Apply

Resources are listed according to the part of the lesson cycle for which they were designed.

Using the Pupil's Edition ___ Concept Check	☐ Pupil's Edition p. 140
Using Support Materials ___ More Practice *10* Application	☐ 📖 Grammar, Usage, and Mechanics Workbook p. 98 ☑ 📖 Grammar, Usage, and Mechanics Workbook p. 99
Using Technology ___ Verbs Forms and Tenses	☐ 💿 Grammar Coach CD-ROM, Lesson 6
Customizing the Lesson ___ Verbs	☐ 🎧 SAE/ESL English Grammar Survival Kit pp. 23–36

Space is provided for inserting approximate times. Resources that you are planning on using can be checked off.

Assess and Close

Ongoing Assessment Options ___ Chapter Mid-point Test ___ Exercise Bank ___ Create a Lesson Quiz	☐ 📖 Assessment Masters p. 29 ☐ Pupil's Edition p. 599 ☐ 💿 Test Generator CD-ROM

Reteach

Using Support Materials ___ Reteaching	

CHAPTER 6

Homework Assignments
_____
_____
_____
_____
_____
_____
_____
_____
_____

Other Teaching Materials
_____
_____
_____
_____
_____
_____
_____
_____
_____

Space is provided for planning homework assignments and for listing additional teaching resources that can be used in conjunction with Language Network.

Tabs make it easy to navigate the book.

Copyright © McDougal Littell Inc.

CHAPTER 1

Preparing for Chapter 1

Resources

Warm-Up
___ Write Away

☐ Pupil's Edition p. 4

Diagnostic Testing
___ Diagnostic Test
___ Chapter Pretest

☐ Pupils' Edition p. 5
☐ 📠 Assessment Masters
    pp. 2–3 or
    💿 Test Generator CD-ROM

(Lesson 1) Nouns

Pages 6–8

Lesson 1 Objectives
To understand what nouns are and to identify them in sentences

Teach

Resources

Warm-Up
___ Test Preparation

☐ 🏛 Daily Test Prep. p. DT1

Using the Pupil's Edition
___ Here's the Idea
___ Why It Matters in Writing

☐ Pupil's Edition p. 6
☐ Pupil's Edition p. 7

Practice and Apply

Using the Pupil's Edition
___ Concept Check
___ Revising

☐ Pupil's Edition p. 8
☐ Pupil's Edition p. 8

Using Support Materials
___ More Practice

___ Application

☐ 📠 Grammar, Usage, and
    Mechanics Workbook p. 2
☐ 📠 Grammar, Usage, and
    Mechanics Workbook p. 3

Customizing the Lesson
___ Countable vs.
    Noncountable Nouns

☐ 🎧 SAE/ESL English Grammar
    Survival Kit pp. 1–2

Assess and Close

Ongoing Assessment Options
___ Exercise Bank
___ Create a Lesson Quiz

☐ Pupil's Edition p. 584
☐ 💿 Test Generator CD-ROM

Reteach

Using Support Materials
___ Reteaching

☐ 📠 Grammar, Usage, and
    Mechanics Workbook p. 1

Homework Assignments

_____
_____
_____
_____
_____
_____
_____
_____

Other Teaching Materials

_____
_____
_____
_____
_____
_____
_____
_____

Lesson 2

Personal and Possessive Pronouns

Pages 9–10

Lesson 2 Objectives
To understand what pesonal pronouns, including their possessive forms, are and to identify them in sentences

Teach	Resources

Warm-Up
___ Test Preparation   □ 📖 Daily Test Prep. p. DT1

Using the Pupil's Edition
___ Here's the Idea   □ Pupil's Edition p. 9
___ Why It Matters in Writing   □ Pupil's Edition p. 9

Practice and Apply

Using the Pupil's Edition
___ Concept Check   □ Pupil's Edition p. 10
___ Revising   □ Pupil's Edition p. 10

Using Support Materials
___ More Practice   □ 🎞 Grammar, Usage, and Mechanics Workbook p. 5

___ Application   □ 🎞 Grammar, Usage, and Mechanics Workbook p. 6

Customizing the Lesson
___ Subject Pronoun Use   □ ◯ SAE/ESL English Grammar Survival Kit pp. 5–8

Assess and Close

Ongoing Assessment Options
___ Exercise Bank   □ Pupil's Edition p. 584
___ Create a Lesson Quiz   □ ⊛ Test Generator CD-ROM

Reteach

Using Support Materials
___ Reteaching   □ 🎞 Grammar, Usage, and Mechanics Workbook p. 4

Homework Assignments
_____
_____
_____
_____
_____
_____
_____
_____
_____

Other Teaching Materials
_____
_____
_____
_____
_____
_____
_____
_____
_____
_____

Copyright © McDougal Littell Inc.

Lesson 3

Other Kinds of Pronouns

Pages 11–13

Lesson 3 Objectives

To understand what reflexive, intensive, demonstrative, indefinite, interrogative, and relative pronouns are and to identify them in sentences

Teach	Resources
Warm-Up	
___ Test Preparation	☐ 📖 Daily Test Prep. p. DT2
Using the Pupil's Edition	
___ Here's the Idea	☐ Pupil's Edition p. 11
___ Why It Matters in Writing	☐ Pupil's Edition p. 12

Practice and Apply

Using the Pupil's Edition	
___ Concept Check	☐ Pupil's Edition p. 13
___ Revising	☐ Pupil's Edition p. 13
Using Support Materials	
___ More Practice	☐ 📖 Grammar, Usage, and Mechanics Workbook p. 8
___ Application	☐ 📖 Grammar, Usage, and Mechanics Workbook p. 9

Assess and Close

Ongoing Assessment Options	
___ Exercise Bank	☐ Pupil's Edition p. 585
___ Create a Lesson Quiz	☐ 💿 Test Generator CD-ROM

Reteach

Using Support Materials	
___ Reteaching	☐ 📖 Grammar, Usage, and Mechanics Workbook p. 7

Homework Assignments

_____
_____
_____
_____
_____
_____
_____

Other Teaching Materials

_____
_____
_____
_____
_____
_____
_____
_____

Lesson 4 **Verbs**

CHAPTER 1

Lesson 4 Objectives
To understand how verbs function and to identify them in sentences

Teach

Resources

Warm-Up
___ Test Preparation

☐ 🏛 Daily Test Prep. p. DT2

Using the Pupil's Edition
___ Here's the Idea
___ Why It Matters in Writing

☐ Pupil's Edition p. 14
☐ Pupil's Edition p. 16

Practice and Apply

Using the Pupil's Edition
___ Concept Check

☐ Pupil's Edition p. 16

Using Support Materials
___ More Practice

☐ 📓 Grammar, Usage, and Mechanics Workbook p. 11

___ Application

☐ 📓 Grammar, Usage, and Mechanics Workbook p. 12

Customizing the Lesson
___ Verbs

☐ ◯ SAE/ESL English Grammar Survival Kit pp. 23–46

Assess and Close

Ongoing Assessment Options
___ Chapter Mid-point Test
___ Exercise Bank
___ Create a Lesson Quiz

☐ 📓 Assessment Masters p. 24
☐ Pupil's Edition p. 585
☐ ⊗ Test Generator CD-ROM

Reteach

Using Support Materials
___ Reteaching

☐ 📓 Grammar, Usage, and Mechanics Workbook p. 10

Homework Assignments

_____
_____
_____
_____
_____
_____
_____
_____
_____
_____

Other Teaching Materials

_____
_____
_____
_____
_____
_____
_____
_____
_____
_____

CHAPTER 1

Lesson 5 Adjectives

Pages 17–19

Lesson 5 Objectives
To understand how adjectives function and to identify and use them in sentences

Teach	Resources
Warm-Up	
___ Test Preparation	☐ 📖 Daily Test Prep. p. DT3
Using the Pupil's Edition	
___ Here's the Idea	☐ Pupil's Edition p. 17
___ Why It Matters in Writing	☐ Pupil's Edition p. 18

Practice and Apply

Using the Pupil's Edition	
___ Concept Check	☐ Pupil's Edition p. 18
___ Revising	☐ Pupil's Edition p. 19
___ Writing	☐ Pupil's Edition p. 19
Using Support Materials	
___ More Practice	☐ 📄 Grammar, Usage, and Mechanics Workbook p. 14
___ Application	☐ 📄 Grammar, Usage, and Mechanics Workbook p. 15
Customizing the Lesson	
___ Adjective Placement	☐ 🎧 SAE/ESL English Grammar Survival Kit pp. 9–10

Assess and Close

Ongoing Assessment Options	
___ Exercise Bank	☐ Pupil's Edition p. 586
___ Create a Lesson Quiz	☐ 💿 Test Generator CD-ROM

Reteach

Using Support Materials	
___ Reteaching	☐ 📄 Grammar, Usage, and Mechanics Workbook p. 13

Homework Assignments
_____
_____
_____
_____
_____
_____
_____
_____

Other Teaching Materials
_____
_____
_____
_____
_____
_____
_____
_____
_____
_____

Lesson 6

Adverbs

Pages 20–22

Lesson 6 Objectives

To understand how adverbs function and to identify and use them in sentences

Teach	Resources
Warm-Up	
___ Test Preparation	☐ 📖 Daily Test Prep. p. DT3
Using the Pupil's Edition	
___ Here's the Idea	☐ Pupil's Edition p. 20
___ Why It Matters in Writing	☐ Pupil's Edition p. 21

Practice and Apply

Using the Pupil's Edition	
___ Concept Check	☐ Pupil's Edition p. 21
___ Revising	☐ Pupil's Edition p. 22
Using Support Materials	
___ More Practice	☐ 📺 Grammar, Usage, and Mechanics Workbook p. 17
___ Application	☐ 📺 Grammar, Usage, and Mechanics Workbook p. 18
Customizing the Lesson	
___ Adjectives vs. Adverbs	☐ 🎧 SAE/ESL English Grammar Survival Kit pp. 11–12

Assess and Close

Ongoing Assessment Options	
___ Exercise Bank	☐ Pupil's Edition p. 586
___ Create a Lesson Quiz	☐ 💿 Test Generator CD-ROM

Reteach

Using Support Materials	
___ Reteaching	☐ 📺 Grammar, Usage, and Mechanics Workbook p. 16

Homework Assignments

_____
_____
_____
_____
_____
_____
_____
_____
_____
_____
_____

Other Teaching Materials

_____
_____
_____
_____
_____
_____
_____
_____
_____
_____
_____

Lesson 7 Prepositions

Pages 23–25

Lesson 7 Objectives

To understand how prepositions function and to identify and use them in sentences

 THE LANGUAGE OF LITERATURE Connect to *The Tragedy of Romeo and Juliet,* Level 9.

Teach	Resources
Warm-Up	
___ Test Preparation	☐ 🏛 Daily Test Prep. p. DT4
Using the Pupil's Edition	
___ Here's the Idea	☐ Pupil's Edition p. 23
___ Why It Matters in Writing	☐ Pupil's Edition p. 24

Practice and Apply

Using the Pupil's Edition	
___ Concept Check	☐ Pupil's Edition p. 25
___ Writing	☐ Pupil's Edition p. 25
Using Support Materials	
___ More Practice	☐ 🖾 Grammar, Usage, and Mechanics Workbook p. 20
___ Application	☐ 🖾 Grammar, Usage, and Mechanics Workbook p. 21
Customizing the Lesson	
___ Prepositions	☐ 🎧 SAE/ESL English Grammar Survival Kit pp. 17–22

Assess and Close

Ongoing Assessment Options	
___ Exercise Bank	☐ Pupil's Edition p. 586
___ Create a Lesson Quiz	☐ ⊛ Test Generator CD-ROM

Reteach

Using Support Materials	
___ Reteaching	☐ 🖾 Grammar, Usage, and Mechanics Workbook p. 19

Homework Assignments

_____
_____
_____
_____
_____
_____
_____
_____
_____

Other Teaching Materials

_____
_____
_____
_____
_____
_____
_____
_____

Lesson 8

Conjunctions

Lesson 8 Objectives
To recognize how conjunctions and conjunctive adverbs function and to identify and use them in sentences

Teach	Resources
Warm-Up	
___ Test Preparation	☐ 🏛 Daily Test Prep. p. DT4
Using the Pupil's Edition	
___ Here's the Idea	☐ Pupil's Edition p. 26
___ Why It Matters in Writing	☐ Pupil's Edition p. 27

Practice and Apply

Using the Pupil's Edition	
___ Concept Check	☐ Pupil's Edition p. 28
___ Writing	☐ Pupil's Edition p. 28
Using Support Materials	
___ More Practice	☐ 🎞 Grammar, Usage, and Mechanics Workbook p. 23
___ Application	☐ 🎞 Grammar, Usage, and Mechanics Workbook p. 24

Assess and Close

Ongoing Assessment Options	
___ Exercise Bank	☐ Pupil's Edition p. 587
___ Create a Lesson Quiz	☐ 💿 Test Generator CD-ROM

Reteach

Using Support Materials	
___ Reteaching	☐ 🎞 Grammar, Usage, and Mechanics Workbook p. 22

Homework Assignments

_____
_____
_____
_____
_____
_____
_____
_____

Other Teaching Materials

_____
_____
_____
_____
_____
_____
_____
_____

Lesson 9

Interjections

Page 29

Lesson 9 Objectives

To recognize how interjections function and to identify and use them in sentences

THE LANGUAGE OF LITERATURE Connect to *The Gift of the Magi*, Level 9.

Teach	**Resources**
Warm-Up	
___ Test Preparation	☐ 🏛 Daily Test Prep. p. DT5
Using the Pupil's Edition	
___ Here's the Idea	☐ Pupil's Edition p. 29
___ Why It Matters in Writing	☐ Pupil's Edition p. 29

Practice and Apply

Using the Pupil's Edition	
___ Concept Check	☐ Pupil's Edition p. 29
Using Support Materials	
___ More Practice	☐ 📖 Grammar, Usage, and Mechanics Workbook p. 23
___ Application	☐ 📖 Grammar, Usage, and Mechanics Workbook p. 24
Customizing the Lesson	
___ Subject Pronoun Use	☐ 🎧 SAE/ESL English Grammar Survival Kit pp. 5–8

Assess and Close

Ongoing Assessment Options	
___ Exercise Bank	☐ Pupil's Edition p. 587
___ Create a Lesson Quiz	☐ 💿 Test Generator CD-ROM

Reteach

Using Support Materials	
___ Reteaching	☐ 📖 Grammar, Usage, and Mechanics Workbook p. 22

Wrapping Up Chapter 1

	Resources
Application and Review	
___ Real World Grammar	☐ Pupil's Edition pp. 30–31
___ Mixed Review	☐ Pupil's Edition p. 32
Assessment	
___ Mastery Test	☐ Pupil's Edition p. 33
___ Chapter Mastery Tests	☐ 📖 Assessment Masters pp. 35–42 or 💿 Test Generator CD-ROM
___ Grammar Chapter Quiz	☐ 🖱 mcdougallittell.com

Homework Assignments

_____
_____
_____
_____
_____
_____
_____
_____

Other Teaching Materials

_____
_____
_____
_____
_____
_____
_____
_____

Preparing for Chapter 2

Resources

Warm-Up
___ Write Away

☐ Pupil's Edition p. 36

Diagnostic Testing
___ Diagnostic Test
___ Chapter Pretest

☐ Pupils' Edition p. 37
☐ 🖼 Assessment Masters
    pp. 4–5 or
⊙ Test Generator CD-ROM

Lesson 1

Simple Subjects and Predicates

Pages 38–40

Lesson 1 Objectives
To recognize the two parts of a sentence—subject and predicate—
and to apply this information in writing

THE LANGUAGE OF
LITERATURE Connect to *The Perfect Storm*, Level 9.

Teach

Resources

Warm-Up
___ Test Preparation

☐ 🏛 Daily Test Prep. p. DT5

Using the Pupil's Edition
___ Here's the Idea
___ Why It Matters in Writing

☐ Pupil's Edition p. 38
☐ Pupil's Edition p. 39

Practice and Apply

Using the Pupil's Edition
___ Concept Check
___ Editing
___ Writing

☐ Pupil's Edition p. 39
☐ Pupil's Edition p. 40
☐ Pupil's Edition p. 40

Using Support Materials
___ More Practice

___ Application

☐ 🖼 Grammar, Usage, and
    Mechanics Workbook p. 26
☐ 🖼 Grammar, Usage, and
    Mechanics Workbook p. 27

Assess and Close

Ongoing Assessment Options
___ Exercise Bank
___ Create a Lesson Quiz

☐ Pupil's Edition p. 588
☐ ⊙ Test Generator CD-ROM

Reteach

Using Support Materials
___ Reteaching

☐ 🖼 Grammar, Usage, and
    Mechanics Workbook p. 25

Homework Assignments

_____
_____
_____
_____
_____
_____
_____
_____
_____

Other Teaching Materials

_____
_____
_____
_____
_____
_____
_____
_____
_____

Lesson 2

Complete Subjects and Predicates

Pages 41–42

Lesson 2 Objectives
To identify and use complete subjects and predicates

Teach	Resources
Warm-Up	
___ Test Preparation	☐ 🏛 Daily Test Prep. p. DT6
Using the Pupil's Edition	
___ Here's the Idea	☐ Pupil's Edition p. 41
___ Why It Matters in Writing	☐ Pupil's Edition p. 41

Practice and Apply

Using the Pupil's Edition	
___ Concept Check	☐ Pupil's Edition p. 42
___ Writing	☐ Pupil's Edition p. 42
Using Support Materials	
___ More Practice	☐ 📖 Grammar, Usage, and Mechanics Workbook p. 29
___ Application	☐ 📖 Grammar, Usage, and Mechanics Workbook p. 30

Assess and Close

Ongoing Assessment Options	
___ Exercise Bank	☐ Pupil's Edition p. 588
___ Create a Lesson Quiz	☐ 💿 Test Generator CD-ROM

Reteach

Using Support Materials	
___ Reteaching	☐ 📖 Grammar, Usage, and Mechanics Workbook p. 28

Homework Assignments

_____
_____
_____
_____
_____
_____
_____
_____
_____
_____

Other Teaching Materials

_____
_____
_____
_____
_____
_____
_____
_____
_____
_____

Lesson 3

Compound Subjects and Verbs

Pages 43–44

Lesson 3 Objectives
To identify compound subjects and verbs and to use them in writing

Teach	Resources
Warm-Up	
___ Test Preparation	☐ 📘 Daily Test Prep. p. DT6
Using the Pupil's Edition	
___ Here's the Idea	☐ Pupil's Edition p. 43
___ Why It Matters in Writing	☐ Pupil's Edition p. 43
Using Support Materials	
___ Combining Sentences	☐ 📘 Visual Grammar™ Tiles, Lesson 1–2

Practice and Apply

Using the Pupil's Edition	
___ Concept Check	☐ Pupil's Edition p. 44
___ Revising	☐ Pupil's Edition p. 44
Using Support Materials	
___ More Practice	☐ 📄 Grammar, Usage, and Mechanics Workbook p. 32
___ Application	☐ 📄 Grammar, Usage, and Mechanics Workbook p. 33

Assess and Close

Ongoing Assessment Options	
___ Exercise Bank	☐ Pupil's Edition p. 589
___ Create a Lesson Quiz	☐ 💿 Test Generator CD-ROM

Reteach

Using Support Materials	
___ Reteaching	☐ 📄 Grammar, Usage, and Mechanics Workbook p. 31

Homework Assignments
_____
_____
_____
_____
_____
_____
_____
_____

Other Teaching Materials
_____
_____
_____
_____
_____
_____
_____
_____

Lesson 4

Kinds of Sentences

Pages 45–46

Lesson 4 Objectives
To recognize the four kinds of sentences and to apply this knowledge in writing

Teach

Warm-Up
___ Test Preparation

Using the Pupil's Edition
___ Here's the Idea
___ Why It Matters in Writing

Practice and Apply

Using the Pupil's Edition
___ Concept Check
___ Writing

Using Support Materials
___ More Practice

___ Application

Assess and Close

Ongoing Assessment Options
___ Chapter Mid-point Test
___ Exercise Bank
___ Create a Lesson Quiz

Reteach

Using Support Materials
___ Reteaching

Resources

☐ Daily Test Prep. p. DT7

☐ Pupil's Edition p. 45
☐ Pupil's Edition p. 45

☐ Pupil's Edition p. 46
☐ Pupil's Edition p. 46

☐ Grammar, Usage, and Mechanics Workbook p. 35
☐ Grammar, Usage, and Mechanics Workbook p. 36

☐ Assessment Masters p. 25
☐ Pupil's Edition p. 589
☐ Test Generator CD-ROM

☐ Grammar, Usage, and Mechanics Workbook p. 34

Homework Assignments

Other Teaching Materials

Lesson 5

Subjects in Unusual Positions

Pages 47–49

Lesson 5 Objectives
To recognize that subjects may appear in unusual positions in a sentence and to apply this knowledge in writing

THE LANGUAGE OF LITERATURE Connect to *Marigolds*, Level 9.

Teach | Resources

Warm-Up
___ Test Preparation   ☐ 🏛 Daily Test Prep. p. DT7

Using the Pupil's Edition
___ Here's the Idea   ☐ Pupil's Edition p. 47
___ Why It Matters in Writing   ☐ Pupil's Edition p. 48

Using Support Materials
___ Subjects in Unusual Positions   ☐ 🏛 Visual Grammar™ Tiles, Lessons 3–5

Practice and Apply

Using the Pupil's Edition
___ Concept Check   ☐ Pupil's Edition p. 49
___ Writing   ☐ Pupil's Edition p. 49

Using Support Materials
___ More Practice   ☐ 📖 Grammar, Usage, and Mechanics Workbook p. 38
___ Application   ☐ 📖 Grammar, Usage, and Mechanics Workbook p. 39

Customizing the Lesson
___ Verbs: Inverted Word Order   ☐ 🎧 SAE/ESL English Grammar Survival Kit pp. 37–38
___ Inverted Sentences   ☐ 📖 Side by Side p. 39

Assess and Close

Ongoing Assessment Options
___ Exercise Bank   ☐ Pupil's Edition p. 590
___ Create a Lesson Quiz   ☐ 💿 Test Generator CD-ROM

Reteach

Using Support Materials
___ Reteaching   ☐ 📖 Grammar, Usage, and Mechanics Workbook p. 37

Homework Assignments
_____
_____
_____
_____
_____
_____
_____
_____
_____

Other Teaching Materials
_____
_____
_____
_____
_____
_____
_____
_____
_____
_____

Subject Complements

Pages 50–51

Lesson 6 Objectives
To identify subject complements and to use them in writing

Teach

Teach	Resources

Warm-Up
___ Test Preparation

☐ 🏛 Daily Test Prep. p. DT8

Using the Pupil's Edition
___ Here's the Idea
___ Why It Matters in Writing

☐ Pupil's Edition p. 50
☐ Pupil's Edition p. 50

Using Support Materials
___ Predicate Nominatives
and Adjectives

☐ 🏛 Visual Grammar™ Tiles,
Lesson 6

Practice and Apply

Using the Pupil's Edition
___ Concept Check
___ Revising

☐ Pupil's Edition p. 51
☐ Pupil's Edition p. 51

Using Support Materials
___ More Practice

☐ 📖 Grammar, Usage, and
Mechanics Workbook p. 41

___ Application

☐ 📖 Grammar, Usage, and
Mechanics Workbook p. 42

Assess and Close

Ongoing Assessment Options
___ Exercise Bank
___ Create a Lesson Quiz

☐ Pupil's Edition p. 590
☐ ⊗ Test Generator CD-ROM

Reteach

Using Support Materials
___ Reteaching

☐ 📖 Grammar, Usage, and
Mechanics Workbook p. 40

Homework Assignments
_____
_____
_____
_____
_____
_____
_____
_____

Other Teaching Materials
_____
_____
_____
_____
_____
_____
_____
_____
_____

Lesson 7

Objects of Verbs

Pages 52–53

Lesson 7 Objectives
To identify objects of verbs and to use them in writing

Teach	Resources
Warm-Up	
___ Test Preparation	☐ 🏛 Daily Test Prep. p. DT8
Using the Pupil's Edition	
___ Here's the Idea	☐ Pupil's Edition p. 52
___ Why It Matters in Writing	☐ Pupil's Edition p. 53

Practice and Apply

Using the Pupil's Edition	
___ Concept Check	☐ Pupil's Edition p. 53
___ Writing	☐ Pupil's Edition p. 53
Using Support Materials	
___ More Practice	☐ 📖 Grammar, Usage, and Mechanics Workbook p. 44
___ Application	☐ 📖 Grammar, Usage, and Mechanics Workbook p. 45

Assess and Close

Ongoing Assessment Options	
___ Exercise Bank	☐ Pupil's Edition p. 590
___ Create a Lesson Quiz	☐ 💿 Test Generator CD-ROM

Reteach

Using Support Materials	
___ Reteaching	☐ 📖 Grammar, Usage, and Mechanics Workbook p. 43

Homework Assignments

_____
_____
_____
_____
_____
_____
_____
_____

Other Teaching Materials

_____
_____
_____
_____
_____
_____
_____
_____
_____

Lesson 8

Sentence Diagramming

Pages 54–57

Lesson 8 Objectives
To understand how a sentence works by visually representing the structure of a sentence

Teach | Resources

Warm-Up
___ Test Preparation

☐ 🏛 Daily Test Prep. p. DT9

Using the Pupil's Edition
___ Here's the Idea

☐ Pupil's Edition p. 54

Practice and Apply

Using the Pupil's Edition
___ Concept Check
___ Mixed Review

☐ Pupil's Edition pp. 55, 57
☐ Pupil's Edition p. 57

Using Support Materials
___ More Practice

☐ 📖 Grammar, Usage, and Mechanics Workbook pp. 46–47

___ Application

☐ 📖 Grammar, Usage, and Mechanics Workbook p. 48

Wrapping Up Chapter 2 | Resources

Application and Review
___ Real World Grammar
___ Mixed Review

☐ Pupil's Edition pp. 58–59
☐ Pupil's Edition p. 60

Assessment
___ Mastery Test
___ Chapter Mastery Tests

☐ Pupil's Edition p. 61
☐ 📑 Assessment Masters pp. 43–48 or
◉ Test Generator CD-ROM

___ Grammar Chapter Quiz

☐ 🖰 mcdougallittell.com

Homework Assignments

_____
_____
_____
_____
_____
_____
_____
_____
_____
_____

Other Teaching Materials

_____
_____
_____
_____
_____
_____
_____
_____
_____
_____
_____

CHAPTER 2

Preparing for Chapter 3

Resources

Warm-Up
___ Write Away

☐ Pupil's Edition p. 64

Diagnostic Testing
___ Diagnostic Test
___ Chapter Pretest

☐ Pupils' Edition p. 65
☐ 📠 Assessment Masters
    pp. 6–7 or
    💿 Test Generator CD-ROM

Chapter Resources
___ Using Phrases

☐ 💿 Power Presentations
    CD-ROM, Lesson 1

Lesson 1 Prepositional Phrases

Pages 66–68

Lesson 1 Objectives
To recognize prepositional phrases and to use them correctly in sentences

THE LANGUAGE OF LITERATURE Connect to *The Most Dangerous Game*, Level 9.

Teach

Resources

Homework Assignments

Warm-Up
___ Test Preparation

☐ 🏛 Daily Test Prep. p. DT9

Using the Pupil's Edition
___ Here's the Idea
___ Why It Matters in Writing

☐ Pupil's Edition p. 66
☐ Pupil's Edition p. 67

Using Support Materials
___ Adverb and Adjective
    Prepositional Phrases

☐ 🏛 Visual Grammar™ Tiles,
    Lesson 7

Practice and Apply

Using the Pupil's Edition
___ Concept Check
___ Revising

☐ Pupil's Edition p. 68
☐ Pupil's Edition p. 68

Other Teaching Materials

Using Support Materials
___ More Practice

___ Application

☐ 📠 Grammar, Usage, and
    Mechanics Workbook p. 50
☐ 📠 Grammar, Usage, and
    Mechanics Workbook p. 51

Using Technology
___ Misplaced and Dangling
    Modifiers

☐ 💿 Grammar Coach CD-ROM,
    Lesson 12

CHAPTER 3

Lesson 1

Prepositional Phrases *(continued)*

Pages 66–68

Assess and Close

Ongoing Assessment Options
___ Exercise Bank
___ Create a Lesson Quiz

Reteach

Using Support Materials
___ Reteaching

Resources

☐ Pupil's Edition p. 591
☐ ⊗ Test Generator CD-ROM

☐ 🖳 Grammar, Usage, and
Mechanics Workbook p. 49

CHAPTER 3

Homework Assignments

_____
_____
_____
_____
_____
_____
_____
_____
_____

Other Teaching Materials

_____
_____
_____
_____
_____
_____
_____
_____
_____

Lesson 2

Appositives and Appositive Phrases

Pages 69–70

Lesson 2 Objectives
To recognize appositives and appositive phrases and to use them in sentences

Teach	Resources
Warm-Up	
___ Test Preparation	☐ 📖 Daily Test Prep. p. DT10
Using the Pupil's Edition	
___ Here's the Idea	☐ Pupil's Edition p. 69
___ Why It Matters in Writing	☐ Pupil's Edition p. 69
Using Support Materials	
___ Appositives and Appositive Phrases	☐ 📖 Visual Grammar™ Tiles, Lesson 8

Practice and Apply

Using the Pupil's Edition	
___ Concept Check	☐ Pupil's Edition p. 70
___ Revising	☐ Pupil's Edition p. 70
Using Support Materials	
___ More Practice	☐ 📖 Grammar, Usage, and Mechanics Workbook p. 53
___ Application	☐ 📖 Grammar, Usage, and Mechanics Workbook p. 54

Assess and Close

Ongoing Assessment Options	
___ Exercise Bank	☐ Pupil's Edition p. 591
___ Create a Lesson Quiz	☐ 💿 Test Generator CD-ROM

Reteach

Using Support Materials	
___ Reteaching	☐ 📖 Grammar, Usage, and Mechanics Workbook p. 52

Homework Assignments

_____
_____
_____
_____
_____
_____
_____
_____

Other Teaching Materials

_____
_____
_____
_____
_____
_____

Verbals: Participial Phrases

Pages 71–73

Lesson 3 Objectives
To recognize participial phrases and to use them in sentences

Teach	Resources
Warm-Up	
___ Test Preparation	☐ 🏛 Daily Test Prep. p. DT10
Using the Pupil's Edition	
___ Here's the Idea	☐ Pupil's Edition p. 71
___ Why It Matters in Writing	☐ Pupil's Edition p. 72
Using Support Materials	
___ Misplaced and Dangling Modifiers	☐ 🏛 Quick-Fix Grammar and Style Charts p. QF10

Practice and Apply

Using the Pupil's Edition	
___ Concept Check	☐ Pupil's Edition p. 73
___ Revising	☐ Pupil's Edition p. 73
Using Support Materials	
___ More Practice	☐ 📖 Grammar, Usage, and Mechanics Workbook p. 56
___ Application	☐ 📖 Grammar, Usage, and Mechanics Workbook p. 57
Using Technology	
___ Misplaced and Dangling Modifiers	☐ 💿 Grammar Coach CD-ROM, Lesson 12

Assess and Close

Ongoing Assessment Options	
___ Chapter Mid-point Test	☐ 📖 Assessment Masters p. 26
___ Exercise Bank	☐ Pupil's Edition p. 592
___ Create a Lesson Quiz	☐ 💿 Test Generator CD-ROM

Reteach

Using Support Materials	
___ Reteaching	☐ 📖 Grammar, Usage, and Mechanics Workbook p. 55

CHAPTER 3

Homework Assignments

_____
_____
_____
_____
_____
_____
_____
_____

Other Teaching Materials

_____
_____
_____
_____
_____
_____
_____
_____
_____

Lesson 4

Verbals: Gerund Phrases

Pages 74–75

Lesson 4 Objectives
To recognize gerund phrases and to use them in sentences

 THE LANGUAGE OF LITERATURE   Connect to *Through the Tunnel*, Level 9.

Teach	Resources
Warm-Up	
___ Test Preparation	☐ 🏛 Daily Test Prep. p. DT11
Using the Pupil's Edition	
___ Here's the Idea	☐ Pupil's Edition p. 74
___ Why It Matters in Writing	☐ Pupil's Edition p. 74
Practice and Apply	
Using the Pupil's Edition	
___ Concept Check	☐ Pupil's Edition p. 75
Using Support Materials	
___ More Practice	☐ 📖 Grammar, Usage, and Mechanics Workbook p. 59
___ Application	☐ 📖 Grammar, Usage, and Mechanics Workbook p. 60
Assess and Close	
Ongoing Assessment Options	
___ Exercise Bank	☐ Pupil's Edition p. 592
___ Create a Lesson Quiz	☐ ⊚ Test Generator CD-ROM
Reteach	
Using Support Materials	
___ Reteaching	☐ 📖 Grammar, Usage, and Mechanics Workbook p. 58

CHAPTER 3

Homework Assignments

_____
_____
_____
_____
_____
_____
_____
_____

Other Teaching Materials

_____
_____
_____
_____
_____
_____
_____

Lesson 5

Verbals: Infinitive Phrases

Pages 76–77

Lesson 5 Objectives
To recognize infinitive phrases and to use them in sentences

Teach	Resources
Warm-Up ___ Test Preparation	☐ 🏛 Daily Test Prep. p. DT11
Using the Pupil's Edition ___ Here's the Idea ___ Why It Matters in Writing	☐ Pupil's Edition p. 76 ☐ Pupil's Edition p. 76

Practice and Apply

Using the Pupil's Edition ___ Concept Check ___ Revising	☐ Pupil's Edition p. 77 ☐ Pupil's Edition p. 77

Using Support Materials
___ More Practice
 	
___ Application
	☐ 📖 Grammar, Usage, and
	    Mechanics Workbook p. 62
	☐ 📖 Grammar, Usage, and
	    Mechanics Workbook p. 63

Assess and Close

Ongoing Assessment Options ___ Exercise Bank ___ Create a Lesson Quiz	☐ Pupil's Edition p. 593 ☐ 💿 Test Generator CD-ROM

Reteach

Using Support Materials ___ Reteaching	☐ 📖 Grammar, Usage, and Mechanics Workbook p. 61

Homework Assignments

_____
_____
_____
_____
_____
_____
_____
_____

Other Teaching Materials

_____
_____
_____
_____
_____
_____
_____
_____

CHAPTER 3

Lesson 6 **Placement of Phrases**   *Pages 78–79*

Lesson 6 Objectives
To recognize correct placement of phrases in sentences and to place phrases correctly when writing sentences

Teach	Resources
Warm-Up	
___ Test Preparation	☐ 🏛 Daily Test Prep. p. DT12
Using the Pupil's Edition	
___ Here's the Idea	☐ Pupil's Edition p. 78
___ Why It Matters in Writing	☐ Pupil's Edition p. 79
Using the Pupil's Edition	
___ Misplaced and Dangling Modifiers	☐ 🏛 Quick-Fix Grammar and Style Charts p. QF10
___ Phrases	☐ 🏛 Visual Grammar™ Tiles, Lessons 9–10

Practice and Apply

Using the Pupil's Edition	
___ Concept Check	☐ Pupil's Edition p. 79
Using Support Materials	
___ More Practice	☐ 📖 Grammar, Usage, and Mechanics Workbook p. 65
___ Application	☐ 📖 Grammar, Usage, and Mechanics Workbook p. 66
Using Technology	
___ Misplaced and Dangling Modifiers	☐ 💿 Grammar Coach CD-ROM, Lesson 12

Assess and Close

Ongoing Assessment Options	
___ Exercise Bank	☐ Pupil's Edition p. 593
___ Create a Lesson Quiz	☐ 💿 Test Generator CD-ROM

Reteach

Using Support Materials	
___ Reteaching	☐ 📖 Grammar, Usage, and Mechanics Workbook p. 64

Homework Assignments
_____
_____
_____
_____
_____
_____
_____
_____
_____

Other Teaching Materials
_____
_____
_____
_____
_____
_____
_____
_____
_____
_____

Lesson 7

Sentence Diagramming

Pages 80–83

Lesson 7 Objectives
To understand how phrases function in sentences and to represent them visually

Teach	Resources
Warm-Up	
___ Test Preparation	☐ 📖 Daily Test Prep. p. DT12
Using the Pupil's Edition	
___ Here's the Idea	☐ Pupil's Edition p. 80

Practice and Apply

Using the Pupil's Edition	
___ Concept Check	☐ Pupil's Edition pp. 80–83
Using Support Materials	
___ More Practice	☐ 📖 Grammar, Usage, and Mechanics Workbook pp. 67–68
___ Application	☐ 📖 Grammar, Usage, and Mechanics Workbook p. 69

Wrapping Up Chapter 3	Resources
Application and Review	
___ Real World Grammar	☐ Pupil's Edition pp. 84–85
___ Mixed Review	☐ Pupil's Edition p. 86
Assessment	
___ Mastery Test	☐ Pupil's Edition p. 87
___ Chapter Mastery Tests	☐ 📖 Assessment Masters pp. 49–54 or 💿 Test Generator CD-ROM
___ Grammar Chapter Quiz	☐ ✎ mcdougallittell.com

CHAPTER 3

Homework Assignments
_____
_____
_____
_____
_____
_____
_____
_____
_____
_____
_____
_____

Other Teaching Materials
_____
_____
_____
_____
_____
_____
_____
_____
_____
_____
_____
_____
_____

Preparing for Chapter 4	**Resources**

Warm-Up
___ Write Away

☐ Pupil's Edition p. 90

Diagnostic Testing
___ Diagnostic Test
___ Chapter Pretest

☐ Pupils' Edition p. 91
☐ 🖾 Assessment Masters
    pp. 8–9 or
    💿 Test Generator CD-ROM

Chapter Resources
___ Using Phrases

☐ 💿 Power Presentations
    CD-ROM, Lesson 2

Lesson 1 — Kinds of Clauses

Pages 6–8

Lesson 1 Objectives
To recognize subordinate and independent clauses and to use them in sentences

Teach	**Resources**

Warm-Up
___ Test Preparation

☐ ⚖ Daily Test Prep. p. DT13

Using the Pupil's Edition
___ Here's the Idea
___ Why It Matters in Writing

☐ Pupil's Edition p. 92
☐ Pupil's Edition p. 93

Practice and Apply

Using the Pupil's Edition
___ Concept Check

☐ Pupil's Edition p. 93

Using Support Materials
___ More Practice

___ Application

☐ 🖾 Grammar, Usage, and
    Mechanics Workbook p. 71
☐ 🖾 Grammar, Usage, and
    Mechanics Workbook p. 72

Assess and Close

Ongoing Assessment Options
___ Exercise Bank
___ Create a Lesson Quiz

☐ Pupil's Edition p. 594
☐ 💿 Test Generator CD-ROM

Reteach

Using Support Materials
___ Reteaching

☐ 🖾 Grammar, Usage, and
    Mechanics Workbook p. 70

Homework Assignments

_____
_____
_____
_____
_____
_____
_____

Other Teaching Materials

_____
_____
_____
_____
_____
_____
_____
_____
_____

CHAPTER 4

Lesson 2

Adjective and Adverb Clauses

Pages 94–97

Lesson 2 Objectives
To recognize modifying clauses and to use them in sentences

Teach	Resources
Warm-Up	
___ Test Preparation	☐ 🏛 Daily Test Prep. p. DT13
Using the Pupil's Edition	
___ Here's the Idea	☐ Pupil's Edition p. 94
___ Why It Matters in Writing	☐ Pupil's Edition p. 96
Using Support Materials	
___ Clauses and Sentence Structure	☐ 🏛 Visual Grammar™ Tiles, Lessons 11–12

Practice and Apply

Using the Pupil's Edition	
___ Concept Check	☐ Pupil's Edition p. 97
___ Revising	☐ Pupil's Edition p. 97
Using Support Materials	
___ More Practice	☐ 🎞 Grammar, Usage, and Mechanics Workbook p. 74
___ Application	☐ 🎞 Grammar, Usage, and Mechanics Workbook p. 75

Assess and Close

Ongoing Assessment Options	
___ Exercise Bank	☐ Pupil's Edition p. 595
___ Create a Lesson Quiz	☐ ⊙ Test Generator CD-ROM

Reteach

Using Support Materials	
___ Reteaching	☐ 🎞 Grammar, Usage, and Mechanics Workbook p. 73

Homework Assignments

_____
_____
_____
_____
_____
_____
_____
_____
_____
_____

Other Teaching Materials

_____
_____
_____
_____
_____
_____
_____
_____
_____
_____

CHAPTER 4

Lesson 3 **Noun Clauses**   *Pages 98–100*

Lesson 3 Objectives
To recognize noun clauses and to use them in sentences

Teach	Resources

Warm-Up
___ Test Preparation   ☐ 🏛 Daily Test Prep. p. DT14

Using the Pupil's Edition
___ Here's the Idea   ☐ Pupil's Edition p. 98
___ Why It Matters in Writing   ☐ Pupil's Edition p. 99

Using Support Materials
___ Noun Clauses as Different   ☐ 🏛 Visual Grammar™ Tiles,
    Parts of Speech   Lesson 13

Practice and Apply

Using the Pupil's Edition
___ Concept Check   ☐ Pupil's Edition p. 99
___ Revising   ☐ Pupil's Edition p. 100
___ Writing   ☐ Pupil's Edition p. 100

Using Support Materials
___ More Practice   ☐ 📖 Grammar, Usage, and
                                           Mechanics Workbook p. 77
___ Application   ☐ 📖 Grammar, Usage, and
                                           Mechanics Workbook p. 78

Assess and Close

Ongoing Assessment Options
___ Chapter Mid-point Test   ☐ 📖 Assessment Masters p. 27
___ Exercise Bank   ☐ Pupil's Edition p. 595
___ Create a Lesson Quiz   ☐ ⊗ Test Generator CD-ROM

Reteach

Using Support Materials
___ Reteaching   ☐ 📖 Grammar, Usage, and
                                           Mechanics Workbook p. 76

Homework Assignments

_____
_____
_____
_____
_____
_____
_____

Other Teaching Materials

_____
_____
_____
_____
_____
_____
_____
_____

CHAPTER 4

Lesson 4 — Sentence Structure

Pages 101–103

Lesson 4 Objectives
To identify and write sentences with various structures

Teach	Resources
Warm-Up	
___ Test Preparation	☐ 🏛 Daily Test Prep. p. DT14
Using the Pupil's Edition	
___ Here's the Idea	☐ Pupil's Edition p. 101
___ Why It Matters in Writing	☐ Pupil's Edition p. 102
Using Support Materials	
___ Sentence Structure	☐ 🏛 Visual Grammar™ Tiles, Lessons 14

Practice and Apply

Using the Pupil's Edition	
___ Concept Check	☐ Pupil's Edition p. 103
___ Revising	☐ Pupil's Edition p. 103
Using Support Materials	
___ More Practice	☐ 🖵 Grammar, Usage, and Mechanics Workbook p. 80
___ Application	☐ 🖵 Grammar, Usage, and Mechanics Workbook p. 81

Assess and Close

Ongoing Assessment Options	
___ Exercise Bank	☐ Pupil's Edition p. 596
___ Create a Lesson Quiz	☐ ⊗ Test Generator CD-ROM

Reteach

Using Support Materials	
___ Reteaching	☐ 🖵 Grammar, Usage, and Mechanics Workbook p. 79

Homework Assignments

_____
_____
_____
_____
_____
_____
_____
_____

Other Teaching Materials

_____
_____
_____
_____
_____
_____
_____
_____
_____

CHAPTER 4

Lesson 5

Sentence Diagramming

Pages 104–107

Lesson 5 Objectives
To recognize the purpose of sentence diagramming and to diagram sentences with various structures

Teach	Resources
Warm-Up ___ Test Preparation	☐ 🏛 Daily Test Prep. p. DT15
Using the Pupil's Edition ___ Here's the Idea	☐ Pupil's Edition p. 104

Practice and Apply

Using the Pupil's Edition ___ Concept Check	☐ Pupil's Edition pp. 104–107
Using Support Materials ___ More Practice	☐ 📖 Grammar, Usage, and Mechanics Workbook p. 82–83
___ Application	☐ 📖 Grammar, Usage, and Mechanics Workbook p. 84

Wrapping Up Chapter 4

	Resources
Application and Review ___ Real World Grammar ___ Mixed Review	☐ Pupil's Edition pp. 108–109 ☐ Pupil's Edition p. 110
Assessment ___ Mastery Test ___ Chapter Mastery Tests	☐ Pupil's Edition p. 111 ☐ 📖 Assessment Masters pp. 55–60 or 💿 Test Generator CD-ROM
___ Grammar Chapter Quiz	☐ 💬 mcdougallittell.com

CHAPTER 4

Homework Assignments
_____
_____
_____
_____
_____
_____
_____
_____

Other Teaching Materials
_____
_____
_____
_____
_____
_____
_____
_____

Preparing for Chapter 5

Resources

Warm-Up
___ Write Away

☐ Pupil's Edition p. 114

Diagnostic Testing
___ Diagnostic Test
___ Chapter Pretest

☐ Pupils' Edition p. 115
☐ 🖳 Assessment Masters
    pp. 10–11 or
    ⊛ Test Generator CD-ROM

Chapter Resources
___ Writing Complete
    Sentences

☐ ⊛ Power Presentations
    CD-ROM Lesson 3

Lesson 1 Sentence Fragments

Pages 116–119

Lesson 1 Objectives
To identify sentence fragments and to correct them in writing

Teach

Resources

Warm-Up
___ Test Preparation

☐ 🏛 Daily Test Prep. p. DT15

Using the Pupil's Edition
___ Here's the Idea
___ Why It Matters in Writing

☐ Pupil's Edition p. 116
☐ Pupil's Edition p. 118

Using Support Materials
___ Sentence Fragments

☐ 🏛 Quick-Fix Grammar and
    Style Charts p. QF1

Practice and Apply

Using the Pupil's Edition
___ Concept Check
___ Revising

☐ Pupil's Edition p. 119
☐ Pupil's Edition p. 119

Using Support Materials
___ More Practice

___ Application

☐ 🖳 Grammar, Usage, and
    Mechanics Workbook p. 86
☐ 🖳 Grammar, Usage, and
    Mechanics Workbook p. 87

Using Technology
___ Sentence Fragments

☐ ⊛ Grammar Coach CD-ROM,
    Lesson 1

Homework Assignments
_____
_____
_____
_____
_____
_____
_____
_____

Other Teaching Materials
_____
_____
_____
_____
_____
_____
_____
_____
_____

CHAPTER 5

Lesson 1

Sentence Fragments *(continued)*

Pages 116–119

Assess and Close

Ongoing Assessment Options
___ Chapter Mid-point Test
___ Exercise Bank
___ Create a Lesson Quiz

Reteach

Using Support Materials
___ Reteaching

Resources

☐ 🖿 Assessment Masters p. 28
☐ Pupil's Edition p. 597
☐ 💿 Test Generator CD-ROM

☐ 🖿 Grammar, Usage, and
　　Mechanics Workbook p. 85

CHAPTER 5

Homework Assignments
_____
_____
_____
_____
_____
_____
_____
_____
_____

Other Teaching Materials
_____
_____
_____
_____
_____
_____
_____
_____
_____

Lesson 2

Run-On Sentences

Pages 120–121

Lesson 2 Objectives
To recognize run-on sentences and to correct them in writing

Teach	Resources
Warm-Up	
___ Test Preparation	☐ 🏛 Daily Test Prep. p. DT16
Using the Pupil's Edition	
___ Here's the Idea	☐ Pupil's Edition p. 120
___ Why It Matters in Writing	☐ Pupil's Edition p. 120
Using Support Materials	
___ Run-On Sentences	☐ 🏛 Quick-Fix Grammar and Style Charts p. QF2

Practice and Apply

Using the Pupil's Edition	
___ Concept Check	☐ Pupil's Edition p. 121
___ Editing	☐ Pupil's Edition p. 121
Using Support Materials	
___ More Practice	☐ 📖 Grammar, Usage, and Mechanics Workbook p. 89
___ Application	☐ 📖 Grammar, Usage, and Mechanics Workbook p. 90
Using Technology	
___ Sentence Fragments	☐ 💿 Grammar Coach CD-ROM, Lesson 2

Assess and Close

Ongoing Assessment Options	
___ Exercise Bank	☐ Pupil's Edition p. 597
___ Create a Lesson Quiz	☐ 💿 Test Generator CD-ROM

Reteach

Using Support Materials	
___ Reteaching	☐ 📖 Grammar, Usage, and Mechanics Workbook p. 88

Homework Assignments

_____
_____
_____
_____
_____
_____
_____
_____
_____

Other Teaching Materials

_____
_____
_____
_____
_____
_____
_____
_____
_____
_____

CHAPTER 5

Lesson 2

Run-On Sentences *(continued)*

Pages 120–121

Wrapping Up Chapter 5

Application and Review
___ Real World Grammar
___ Mixed Review

Assessment
___ Mastery Test
___ Chapter Mastery Tests

___ Grammar Chapter Quiz

Resources

☐ Pupil's Edition pp. 122–123
☐ Pupil's Edition p. 124

☐ Pupil's Edition p. 125
☐ 📖 Assessment Masters
    pp. 61–64 or
    💿 Test Generator CD-ROM
☐ 🖥 mcdougallittell.com

CHAPTER 5

Homework Assignments

_____
_____
_____
_____
_____
_____
_____
_____
_____
_____

Other Teaching Materials

_____
_____
_____
_____
_____
_____
_____
_____
_____
_____

Teacher _____ Class _____ Date _____

Preparing for Chapter 6

Warm-Up
___ Write Away

Diagnostic Testing
___ Diagnostic Test
___ Chapter Pretest

Chapter Resources
___ Using Verbs

Resources

☐ Pupil's Edition p. 128

☐ Pupils' Edition p. 129
☐ 🖿 Assessment Masters
pp. 12–13 or
💿 Test Generator CD-ROM

☐ 💿 Power Presentations
CD-ROM Lesson 4

Lesson 1

The Principal Parts of a Verb

Pages 130–133

Lesson 1 Objectives
To recognize the principal parts of a verb and to use them in writing

Teach

Resources

Warm-Up
___ Test Preparation

Using the Pupil's Edition
___ Here's the Idea
___ Why It Matters in Writing

Using Support Materials
___ Verb Forms and Tenses

☐ 🖿 Daily Test Prep. p. DT16

☐ Pupil's Edition p. 130
☐ Pupil's Edition p. 132

☐ 🖿 Quick-Fix Grammar and
Style Charts p. QF9

Practice and Apply

Using the Pupil's Edition
___ Concept Check
___ Writing

Using Support Materials
___ More Practice

___ Application

Using Technology
___ Verbs Forms and Tenses

☐ Pupil's Edition p. 133
☐ Pupil's Edition p. 133

☐ 🖿 Grammar, Usage, and
Mechanics Workbook p. 92
☐ 🖿 Grammar, Usage, and
Mechanics Workbook p. 93

☐ 💿 Grammar Coach CD-ROM,
Lesson 6

Homework Assignments
_____
_____
_____
_____
_____
_____
_____
_____
_____
_____

Other Teaching Materials
_____
_____
_____
_____
_____
_____
_____
_____
_____
_____

CH

Lesson 1 # The Principal Parts of a Verb *(continued)*   *Pages 130–133*

Assess and Close

Ongoing Assessment Options
___ Exercise Bank
___ Create a Lesson Quiz

Reteach

Using Support Materials
___ Reteaching

Resources

☐ Pupil's Edition p. 598
☐ ⊛ Test Generator CD-ROM

☐ 🖫 Grammar, Usage, and
   Mechanics Workbook p. 91

Homework Assignments

_____
_____
_____
_____
_____
_____
_____
_____
_____

Other Teaching Materials

_____
_____
_____
_____
_____
_____
_____
_____
_____

CHAPTER 6

Teacher _____ Class _____ Date _____

Lesson 2 · Forming Verb Tenses

Pages 134–136

Lesson 2 Objectives
To recognize the forms of various verb tenses and to use them
in writing

THE LANGUAGE OF LITERATURE Connect to *Sorry, Right Number,* Level 9.

Teach	Resources

Warm-Up
___ Test Preparation

☐ 📘 Daily Test Prep. p. DT17

Using the Pupil's Edition
___ Here's the Idea
___ Why It Matters in Writing

☐ Pupil's Edition p. 134
☐ Pupil's Edition p. 136

Using Support Materials
___ Forming Tenses

☐ 📗 Visual Grammar™ Tiles,
　　Lesson 15

Practice and Apply

Using the Pupil's Edition
___ Concept Check

☐ Pupil's Edition p. 136

Using Support Materials
___ More Practice

☐ 📓 Grammar, Usage, and
　　Mechanics Workbook p. 95

___ Application

☐ 📓 Grammar, Usage, and
　　Mechanics Workbook p. 96

Using Technology
___ Verbs Forms and Tenses

☐ 💿 Grammar Coach CD-ROM,
　　Lesson 6

Assess and Close

Ongoing Assessment Options
___ Exercise Bank
___ Create a Lesson Quiz

☐ Pupil's Edition p. 599
☐ 💿 Test Generator CD-ROM

Reteach

Using Support Materials
___ Reteaching

☐ 📓 Grammar, Usage, and
　　Mechanics Workbook p. 94

Homework Assignments

_____
_____
_____
_____
_____
_____
_____
_____

Other Teaching Materials

_____
_____
_____
_____
_____
_____
_____
_____
_____
_____

CHAPTER 6

Lesson 3 **Using Verb Tenses**   *Pages 137–141*

Lesson 3 Objectives
To recognize verb tenses and to use them in writing

 THE LANGUAGE OF LITERATURE   Connect to *Into Thin Air,* Level 9.

Teach	**Resources**
Warm-Up	
___ Test Preparation	☐ 🏛 Daily Test Prep. p. DT17
Using the Pupil's Edition	
___ Here's the Idea	☐ Pupil's Edition p. 137
___ Why It Matters in Writing	☐ Pupil's Edition p. 140

Practice and Apply

Using the Pupil's Edition	
___ Concept Check	☐ Pupil's Edition p. 140
Using Support Materials	
___ More Practice	☐ 🖾 Grammar, Usage, and Mechanics Workbook p. 98
___ Application	☐ 🖾 Grammar, Usage, and Mechanics Workbook p. 99
Using Technology	
___ Verbs Forms and Tenses	☐ 💿 Grammar Coach CD-ROM, Lesson 6
Customizing the Lesson	
___ Verbs	☐ 🎧 SAE/ESL English Grammar Survival Kit pp. 23–36

Assess and Close

Ongoing Assessment Options	
___ Chapter Mid-point Test	☐ 🖾 Assessment Masters p. 29
___ Exercise Bank	☐ Pupil's Edition p. 599
___ Create a Lesson Quiz	☐ 💿 Test Generator CD-ROM

Reteach

Using Support Materials	
___ Reteaching	☐ 🖾 Grammar, Usage, and Mechanics Workbook p. 97

Homework Assignments
_____
_____
_____
_____
_____
_____
_____
_____

Other Teaching Materials
_____
_____
_____
_____
_____
_____
_____
_____
_____
_____

CHAPTER 6

Copyright © McDougal Littell Inc.

Lesson 4

Shifts in Tense

Pages 142–143

Lesson 4 Objectives
To recognize correct shifts in tense within a sentence and to use them in writing

Teach	Resources
Warm-Up	
___ Test Preparation	☐ 📖 Daily Test Prep. p. DT18
Using the Pupil's Edition	
___ Here's the Idea	☐ Pupil's Edition p. 142
___ Why It Matters in Writing	☐ Pupil's Edition p. 142
Using Support Materials	
___ Verb Forms and Tenses	☐ 📖 Quick-Fix Grammar and Style Charts p. QF9

Practice and Apply

Using the Pupil's Edition	
___ Concept Check	☐ Pupil's Edition p. 143
Using Support Materials	
___ More Practice	☐ 📘 Grammar, Usage, and Mechanics Workbook p. 101
___ Application	☐ 📘 Grammar, Usage, and Mechanics Workbook p. 102
Using Technology	
___ Verbs Forms and Tenses	☐ 💿 Grammar Coach CD-ROM, Lesson 6

Assess and Close

Ongoing Assessment Options	
___ Exercise Bank	☐ Pupil's Edition p. 600
___ Create a Lesson Quiz	☐ 💿 Test Generator CD-ROM

Reteach

Using Support Materials	
___ Reteaching	☐ 📘 Grammar, Usage, and Mechanics Workbook p. 100

Homework Assignments

_____
_____
_____
_____
_____
_____
_____
_____

Other Teaching Materials

_____
_____
_____
_____
_____
_____
_____
_____
_____

CHAPTER 6

Lesson 5

Active and Passive Voice

Pages 144–145

Lesson 5 Objectives
To recognize and use verbs in the active and passive voice

Teach	Resources

Teach

Warm-Up
___ Test Preparation

☐ 🏛 Daily Test Prep. p. DT18

Using the Pupil's Edition
___ Here's the Idea
___ Why It Matters in Writing

☐ Pupil's Edition p. 144
☐ Pupil's Edition p. 144

Using Support Materials
___ Verb Forms and Tenses

☐ 🏛 Quick-Fix Grammar and Style Charts p. QF12

___ Passive Voice

☐ 🏛 Visual Grammar™ Tiles, Lesson 16

Practice and Apply

Using the Pupil's Edition
___ Concept Check

☐ Pupil's Edition p. 145

Using Support Materials
___ More Practice

☐ 📓 Grammar, Usage, and Mechanics Workbook p. 104

___ Application

☐ 📓 Grammar, Usage, and Mechanics Workbook p. 105

Using Technology
___ Verbs Forms and Tenses

☐ 💿 Grammar Coach CD-ROM, Lesson 6

Assess and Close

Ongoing Assessment Options
___ Exercise Bank
___ Create a Lesson Quiz

☐ Pupil's Edition p. 601
☐ 💿 Test Generator CD-ROM

Reteach

Using Support Materials
___ Reteaching

☐ 📓 Grammar, Usage, and Mechanics Workbook p. 103

Homework Assignments
_____
_____
_____
_____
_____
_____
_____
_____
_____

Other Teaching Materials
_____
_____
_____
_____
_____
_____
_____
_____

CHAPTER 6

Copyright © McDougal Littell Inc.

Lesson 6

The Mood of a Verb

Pages 146–147

Lesson 6 Objectives
To recognize and use all moods of verbs

THE LANGUAGE OF LITERATURE Connect to *Two Kinds,* and *The Osage Orange Tree,* Level 9.

Teach	Resources
Warm-Up	
___ Test Preparation	☐ 🏛 Daily Test Prep. p. DT19
Using the Pupil's Edition	
___ Here's the Idea	☐ Pupil's Edition p. 146
___ Why It Matters in Writing	☐ Pupil's Edition p. 146

Practice and Apply

Using the Pupil's Edition	
___ Concept Check	☐ Pupil's Edition p. 147
Using Support Materials	
___ More Practice	☐ 📓 Grammar, Usage, and Mechanics Workbook p. 107
___ Application	☐ 📓 Grammar, Usage, and Mechanics Workbook p. 108
Customizing the Lesson	
___ Verbs: Modals	☐ 🎧 SAE/ESL English Grammar Survival Kit pp. 45–46

Assess and Close

Ongoing Assessment Options	
___ Exercise Bank	☐ Pupil's Edition p. 601
___ Create a Lesson Quiz	☐ 💿 Test Generator CD-ROM

Reteach

Using Support Materials	
___ Reteaching	☐ 📓 Grammar, Usage, and Mechanics Workbook p. 106

Homework Assignments

_____
_____
_____
_____
_____
_____
_____
_____

Other Teaching Materials

_____
_____
_____
_____
_____
_____
_____
_____
_____

CHAPTER 6

Lesson 7

Commonly Confused Verbs

Pages 148–149

Lesson 7 Objectives
To distinguish between commonly confused verbs and to use them correctly in writing

Teach

Warm-Up
___ Test Preparation

Using the Pupil's Edition
___ Here's the Idea
___ Why It Matters in Writing

Practice and Apply

Using the Pupil's Edition
___ Concept Check

Using Support Materials
___ More Practice

___ Application

Assess and Close

Ongoing Assessment Options
___ Exercise Bank
___ Create a Lesson Quiz

Reteach

Using Support Materials
___ Reteaching

Resources

☐ 📖 Daily Test Prep. p. DT19

☐ Pupil's Edition p. 148
☐ Pupil's Edition p. 149

☐ Pupil's Edition p. 149

☐ 📖 Grammar, Usage, and Mechanics Workbook p. 110
☐ 📖 Grammar, Usage, and Mechanics Workbook p. 111

☐ Pupil's Edition p. 602
☐ ⊛ Test Generator CD-ROM

☐ 📖 Grammar, Usage, and Mechanics Workbook p. 109

Wrapping Up Chapter 6

Application and Review
___ Real World Grammar
___ Mixed Review

Assessment
___ Mastery Test
___ Chapter Mastery Tests

___ Grammar Chapter Quiz

Resources

☐ Pupil's Edition pp. 150–151
☐ Pupil's Edition p. 152

☐ Pupil's Edition p. 153
☐ 📖 Assessment Masters pp. 65–70 or
⊛ Test Generator CD-ROM
☐ 📖 mcdougallittell.com

Homework Assignments
_____
_____
_____
_____
_____
_____
_____
_____
_____

Other Teaching Materials
_____
_____
_____
_____
_____
_____
_____
_____
_____

CHAPTER 6

Preparing for Chapter 7

Resources

Warm-Up
___ Write Away

☐ Pupil's Edition p. 156

Diagnostic Testing
___ Diagnostic Test
___ Chapter Pretest

☐ Pupils' Edition p. 157
☐ 📠 Assessment Masters
    pp. 14–15 or
  💿 Test Generator CD-ROM

Chapter Resources
___ Subject–Verb Agreement

☐ 💿 Power Presentations
    CD-ROM, Lesson 5

Lesson 1 — Agreement in Number

Pages 158–159

Lesson 1 Objectives
To recognize subject-verb agreement problems in sentences
To revise sentences so that subjects and verbs agree in number

Teach

Resources

Warm-Up
___ Test Preparation

☐ 🏛 Daily Test Prep. p. DT20

Using the Pupil's Edition
___ Here's the Idea
___ Why It Matters in Writing

☐ Pupil's Edition p. 158
☐ Pupil's Edition p. 158

Practice and Apply

Using the Pupil's Edition
___ Concept Check
___ Editing

☐ Pupil's Edition p. 159
☐ Pupil's Edition p. 159

Using Support Materials
___ More Practice

___ Application

☐ 📖 Grammar, Usage, and
    Mechanics Workbook p. 113
☐ 📖 Grammar, Usage, and
    Mechanics Workbook p. 114

Assess and Close

Ongoing Assessment Options
___ Exercise Bank
___ Create a Lesson Quiz

☐ Pupil's Edition p. 602
☐ 💿 Test Generator CD-ROM

Reteach

Using Support Materials
___ Reteaching

☐ 📖 Grammar, Usage, and
    Mechanics Workbook p. 112

Homework Assignments

_____
_____
_____
_____
_____
_____
_____
_____
_____

Other Teaching Materials

_____
_____
_____
_____
_____
_____
_____
_____

Lesson 2

Words Between Subject and Verb

Pages 160–161

Lesson 2 Objectives

To identify subjects and verbs separated by other words

To correct errors in agreement when subjects and verbs are separated by other words

Teach	Resources
Warm-Up	
___ Test Preparation	☐ 🏛 Daily Test Prep. p. DT20
Using the Pupil's Edition	
___ Here's the Idea	☐ Pupil's Edition p. 160
___ Why It Matters in Writing	☐ Pupil's Edition p. 160
Using Support Materials	
___ Subject-Verb Agreement I	☐ 🏛 Quick-Fix Grammar and Style Charts p. QF3
___ Words Between Subject and Verb	☐ 🏛 Visual Grammar™ Tiles, Lesson 17

Practice and Apply

Using the Pupil's Edition	
___ Concept Check	☐ Pupil's Edition p. 161
___ Proofreading	☐ Pupil's Edition p. 161
Using Support Materials	
___ More Practice	☐ 🖼 Grammar, Usage, and Mechanics Workbook p. 116
___ Application	☐ 🖼 Grammar, Usage, and Mechanics Workbook p. 117
Using Technology	
___ Subject and Verb Agreement I	☐ 💿 Grammar Coach CD-ROM, Lesson 4

Assess and Close

Ongoing Assessment Options	
___ Exercise Bank	☐ Pupil's Edition p. 603
___ Create a Lesson Quiz	☐ 💿 Test Generator CD-ROM

Reteach

Using Support Materials	
___ Reteaching	☐ 🖼 Grammar, Usage, and Mechanics Workbook p. 115

Homework Assignments

_____
_____
_____
_____
_____
_____
_____
_____
_____

Other Teaching Materials

_____
_____
_____
_____
_____
_____
_____
_____
_____

CHAPTER 7

Lesson 3

Indefinite-Pronoun Subjects

Pages 162–163

Lesson 3 Objectives
To identify singular and plural indefinite pronouns
To use verbs that agree with indefinite pronoun subjects

Teach | Resources

Warm-Up
___ Test Preparation
☐ 🏛 Daily Test Prep. p. DT21

Using the Pupil's Edition
___ Here's the Idea
___ Why It Matters in Writing
☐ Pupil's Edition p. 162
☐ Pupil's Edition p. 162

Using Support Materials
___ Subject-Verb Agreement II
☐ 🏛 Quick-Fix Grammar and Style Charts p. QF3

___ Compound Subjects
☐ 🏛 Visual Grammar™ Tiles, Lesson 18

Practice and Apply

Using the Pupil's Edition
___ Concept Check
___ Editing
☐ Pupil's Edition p. 163
☐ Pupil's Edition p. 163

Using Support Materials
___ More Practice
☐ 📖 Grammar, Usage, and Mechanics Workbook p. 119

___ Application
☐ 📖 Grammar, Usage, and Mechanics Workbook p. 120

Using Technology
___ Subject and Verb Agreement I
☐ 💿 Grammar Coach CD-ROM, Lesson 4

Assess and Close

Ongoing Assessment Options
___ Chapter Mid-point Test
___ Exercise Bank
___ Create a Lesson Quiz
☐ 📖 Assessment Masters p. 30
☐ Pupil's Edition p. 603
☐ 💿 Test Generator CD-ROM

Reteach

Using Support Materials
___ Reteaching
☐ 📖 Grammar, Usage, and Mechanics Workbook p. 118

Homework Assignments
_____
_____
_____
_____
_____
_____
_____
_____
_____

Other Teaching Materials
_____
_____
_____
_____
_____
_____
_____
_____
_____

CHAPTER 7

Lesson 4

Compound Subjects

Pages 164–165

Lesson 4 Objectives
To identify singular and plural compound subjects
To use verbs that agree with compound subjects

Teach	Resources
Warm-Up	
___ Test Preparation	☐ 🏛 Daily Test Prep. p. DT21
Using the Pupil's Edition	
___ Here's the Idea	☐ Pupil's Edition p. 164
___ Why It Matters in Writing	☐ Pupil's Edition p. 164
Using Support Materials	
___ Subject-Verb Agreement 1–2	☐ 🏛 Quick-Fix Grammar and Style Charts pp. QF3–4
___ Compound Subjects	☐ 🏛 Visual Grammar™ Tiles, Lesson 19

Practice and Apply

Using the Pupil's Edition	
___ Concept Check	☐ Pupil's Edition p. 165
___ Proofreading	☐ Pupil's Edition p. 165
Using Support Materials	
___ More Practice	☐ 🖥 Grammar, Usage, and Mechanics Workbook p. 122
___ Application	☐ 🖥 Grammar, Usage, and Mechanics Workbook p. 123
Using Technology	
___ Subject and Verb Agreement I	☐ ⊛ Grammar Coach CD-ROM, Lesson 4

Assess and Close

Ongoing Assessment Options	
___ Exercise Bank	☐ Pupil's Edition p. 604
___ Create a Lesson Quiz	☐ ⊛ Test Generator CD-ROM

Reteach

Using Support Materials	
___ Reteaching	☐ 🖥 Grammar, Usage, and Mechanics Workbook p. 121

Homework Assignments

_____
_____
_____
_____
_____
_____
_____
_____

Other Teaching Materials

_____
_____
_____
_____
_____
_____
_____
_____
_____
_____

CHAPTER 7

Lesson 5

Other Problem Subjects

Pages 166–168

Lesson 5 Objectives
To identify singular and plural compound subjects
To use verbs that agree with problem subjects

Teach | ## Resources

Warm-Up
___ Test Preparation

☐ 🏛 Daily Test Prep. p. DT22

Using the Pupil's Edition
___ Here's the Idea
___ Why It Matters in Writing

☐ Pupil's Edition p. 166
☐ Pupil's Edition p. 167

Using Support Materials
___ Subject-Verb
    Agreement 2

☐ 🏛 Quick-Fix Grammar and
    Style Charts p. QF4

Practice and Apply

Using the Pupil's Edition
___ Concept Check
___ Proofreading

☐ Pupil's Edition p. 168
☐ Pupil's Edition p. 168

Using Support Materials
___ More Practice

☐ 📖 Grammar, Usage, and
    Mechanics Workbook p. 125

___ Application

☐ 📖 Grammar, Usage, and
    Mechanics Workbook p. 126

Using Technology
___ Subject and Verb
    Agreement II

☐ 💿 Grammar Coach CD-ROM,
    Lesson 5

Assess and Close

Ongoing Assessment Options
___ Exercise Bank
___ Create a Lesson Quiz

☐ Pupil's Edition p. 604
☐ 💿 Test Generator CD-ROM

Reteach

Using Support Materials
___ Reteaching

☐ 📖 Grammar, Usage, and
    Mechanics Workbook p. 121

Homework Assignments
_____
_____
_____
_____
_____
_____
_____
_____
_____
_____

Other Teaching Materials
_____
_____
_____
_____
_____
_____
_____
_____
_____

CHAPTER 7

Lesson 6

Agreement Problems in Sentences

Pages 169–171

Lesson 6 Objectives
To identify the subject and verb in sentences with special problems; to make the subject and verb agree in number

 THE LANGUAGE OF LITERATURE Connect to *Trifles*, Level 9.

Teach	Resources
Warm-Up	
___ Test Preparation	☐ ⚏ Daily Test Prep. p. DT22
Using the Pupil's Edition	
___ Here's the Idea	☐ Pupil's Edition p. 169
___ Why It Matters in Writing	☐ Pupil's Edition p. 170
Using Support Materials	
___ Subject-Verb Agreement 2	☐ ⚏ Quick-Fix Grammar and Style Charts p. QF4
___ Relative Pronouns	☐ ⚏ Visual Grammar™ Tiles, Lesson 20

Practice and Apply

Using the Pupil's Edition	
___ Concept Check	☐ Pupil's Edition p. 170
___ Editing and Proofreading	☐ Pupil's Edition p. 171
Using Support Materials	
___ More Practice	☐ ▤ Grammar, Usage, and Mechanics Workbook p. 128
___ Application	☐ ▤ Grammar, Usage, and Mechanics Workbook p. 129
Using Technology	
___ Subject and Verb Agreement 2	☐ ◉ Grammar Coach CD-ROM, Lesson 5

Assess and Close

Ongoing Assessment Options	
___ Exercise Bank	☐ Pupil's Edition p. 605
___ Create a Lesson Quiz	☐ ◉ Test Generator CD-ROM

Reteach

Using Support Materials	
___ Reteaching	☐ ▤ Grammar, Usage, and Mechanics Workbook p. 127

Homework Assignments

_____
_____
_____
_____
_____
_____
_____
_____

Other Teaching Materials

_____
_____
_____
_____
_____
_____
_____

CHAPTER 7

Lesson 6

Agreement Problems in Sentences *(continued)*   *Pages 169–171*

Wrapping Up Chapter 7

Resources

Application and Review
___ Real World Grammar
___ Mixed Review

☐ Pupil's Edition pp. 172–173
☐ Pupil's Edition p. 174

Assessment
___ Mastery Test
___ Chapter Mastery Tests

☐ Pupil's Edition p. 175
☐ 📖 Assessment Masters
    pp. 71–76 or
    💿 Test Generator CD-ROM

___ Grammar Chapter Quiz

☐ 🔗 mcdougallittell.com

Homework Assignments

_____
_____
_____
_____
_____
_____
_____
_____

Other Teaching Materials

_____
_____
_____
_____
_____
_____
_____
_____

CHAPTER 7

Preparing for Chapter 8

Resources

Warm-Up
___ Write Away

☐ Pupil's Edition p. 178

Diagnostic Testing
___ Diagnostic Test
___ Chapter Pretest

☐ Pupils' Edition p. 179
☐ 📖 Assessment Masters
pp. 16–17 or
💿 Test Generator CD-ROM

Chapter Resources
___ Using Pronouns

☐ 💿 Power Presentations
CD-ROM Lesson 6

Lesson 1 — Pronoun Cases

Page 180

Lesson 1 Objectives

To recognize and use personal pronouns in both numbers and all cases

THE LANGUAGE OF **LITERATURE** Connect to the *Odyssey,* Level 9.

Teach

Resources

Warm-Up
___ Test Preparation

☐ 🏛 Daily Test Prep. p. DT23

Using the Pupil's Edition
___ Here's the Idea
___ Why It Matters in Writing

☐ Pupil's Edition p. 180
☐ Pupil's Edition p. 180

Practice and Apply

Using Support Materials
___ More Practice

☐ 📖 Grammar, Usage, and
Mechanics Workbook p. 131

___ Application

☐ 📖 Grammar, Usage, and
Mechanics Workbook p. 132

Using Technology
___ Pronoun Case

☐ 💿 Grammar Coach CD-ROM,
Lesson 9

Assess and Close

Ongoing Assessment Options
___ Assessment Information

☐ 📖 Teacher's Guide to Assessment and Portfolio Use

Reteach

Using Support Materials
___ Reteaching

☐ 📖 Grammar, Usage, and
Mechanics Workbook p. 130

Homework Assignments
_____
_____
_____
_____
_____
_____
_____
_____
_____

Other Teaching Materials
_____
_____
_____
_____
_____
_____
_____
_____
_____
_____

CHAPTER 8

Lesson 2

Nominative and Objective Cases

Pages 181–184

Lesson 2 Objectives
To recognize pronouns in the nominative and objective cases
To use correct pronoun cases in sentences

Teach

Teach	Resources

Warm-Up
___ Test Preparation

☐ 📖 Daily Test Prep. p. DT23

Using the Pupil's Edition
___ Here's the Idea
___ Why It Matters in Writing

☐ Pupil's Edition p. 181
☐ Pupil's Edition p. 183

Using Support Materials
___ Incorrect Pronoun Case

☐ 📖 Quick-Fix Grammar and
　　 Style Charts p. QF6

Practice and Apply

Using the Pupil's Edition
___ Concept Check
___ Revising
___ Writing

☐ Pupil's Edition p. 183
☐ Pupil's Edition p. 184
☐ Pupil's Edition p. 184

Using Support Materials
___ More Practice

☐ 📖 Grammar, Usage, and
　　 Mechanics Workbook p. 131

___ Application

☐ 📖 Grammar, Usage, and
　　 Mechanics Workbook p. 132

Using Technology
___ Pronoun Case

☐ 💿 Grammar Coach CD-ROM,
　　 Lesson 9

Customizing the Lesson
___ Pronouns

☐ 🎧 SAE/ESL English Grammar
　　 Survival Kit pp. 5–8

Assess and Close

Ongoing Assessment Options
___ Exercise Bank
___ Create a Lesson Quiz

☐ Pupil's Edition p. 606
☐ 💿 Test Generator CD-ROM

Reteach

Using Support Materials
___ Reteaching

☐ 📖 Grammar, Usage, and
　　 Mechanics Workbook p. 130

Homework Assignments

_____
_____
_____
_____
_____
_____
_____
_____

Other Teaching Materials

_____
_____
_____
_____
_____
_____
_____
_____

CHAPTER 8

Lesson 3 — Possessive Case

Pages 185–186

Lesson 3 Objectives
To recognize pronouns in the possessive case
To identify possessive pronouns in sentences and to distinguish
 them from soundalike contractions

Teach	Resources
Warm-Up	
___ Test Preparation	☐ 🏛 Daily Test Prep. p. DT24
Using the Pupil's Edition	
___ Here's the Idea	☐ Pupil's Edition p. 185
___ Why It Matters in Writing	☐ Pupil's Edition p. 186

Practice and Apply

Using the Pupil's Edition	
___ Concept Check	☐ Pupil's Edition p. 186
___ Proofreading	☐ Pupil's Edition p. 186
Using Support Materials	
___ More Practice	☐ 📖 Grammar, Usage, and Mechanics Workbook p. 134
___ Application	☐ 📖 Grammar, Usage, and Mechanics Workbook p. 135
Using Technology	
___ Pronoun Case	☐ 💿 Grammar Coach CD-ROM, Lesson 9

Assess and Close

Ongoing Assessment Options	
___ Exercise Bank	☐ Pupil's Edition p. 606
___ Create a Lesson Quiz	☐ 💿 Test Generator CD-ROM

Reteach

Using Support Materials	
___ Reteaching	☐ 📖 Grammar, Usage, and Mechanics Workbook p. 133

Homework Assignments

_____
_____
_____
_____
_____
_____
_____
_____
_____
_____

Other Teaching Materials

_____
_____
_____
_____
_____
_____
_____
_____
_____
_____

CHAPTER 8

Lesson 4

Using *Who* and *Whom*

Pages 187–189

Lesson 4 Objectives
To recognize the proper use of forms of *who* and *whoever*
To use forms of *who* and *whoever* correctly in sentences

Teach

Resources

Warm-Up
___ Test Preparation
☐ 🏛 Daily Test Prep. p. DT24

Using the Pupil's Edition
___ Here's the Idea
☐ Pupil's Edition p. 187
___ Why It Matters in Writing
☐ Pupil's Edition p. 188

Using Support Materials
___ *Who* and *Whom*
☐ 🏛 Quick-Fix Grammar and
Style Charts p. QF7

___ Pronouns
☐ 🏛 Visual Grammar™ Tiles,
Lessons 21–22

Practice and Apply

Using the Pupil's Edition
___ Concept Check
☐ Pupil's Edition p. 189
___ Proofreading
☐ Pupil's Edition p. 189

Using Support Materials
___ More Practice
☐ 📖 Grammar, Usage, and
Mechanics Workbook p. 137
___ Application
☐ 📖 Grammar, Usage, and
Mechanics Workbook p. 138

Using Technology
___ *Who* and *Whom*
☐ 💿 Grammar Coach CD-ROM,
Lesson 10

Assess and Close

Ongoing Assessment Options
___ Chapter Mid-point Test
☐ 📖 Assessment Masters p. 31
___ Exercise Bank
☐ Pupil's Edition p. 607
___ Create a Lesson Quiz
☐ 💿 Test Generator CD-ROM

Reteach

Using Support Materials
___ Reteaching
☐ 📖 Grammar, Usage, and
Mechanics Workbook p. 136

Homework Assignments

_____
_____
_____
_____
_____
_____
_____
_____
_____

Other Teaching Materials

_____
_____
_____
_____
_____
_____
_____
_____
_____
_____
_____

CHAPTER 8

Pronoun-Antecedent Agreement

Lesson 5

Pages 190–192

Lesson 5 Objectives
To recognize the ways that pronouns must agree with their antecedents

To use correct pronoun-antecedent agreement in writing

Teach	Resources
Warm-Up	
___ Test Preparation	☐ 🏛 Daily Test Prep. p. DT25
Using the Pupil's Edition	
___ Here's the Idea	☐ Pupil's Edition p. 190
___ Why It Matters in Writing	☐ Pupil's Edition p. 191

Practice and Apply

Using the Pupil's Edition	
___ Concept Check	☐ Pupil's Edition p. 192
___ Revising	☐ Pupil's Edition p. 192
Using Support Materials	
___ More Practice	☐ 📄 Grammar, Usage, and Mechanics Workbook p. 140
___ Application	☐ 📄 Grammar, Usage, and Mechanics Workbook p. 141
Using Technology	
___ Pronoun Antecedent Agreement I–II	☐ 💿 Grammar Coach CD-ROM, Lesson 7–8

Assess and Close

Ongoing Assessment Options	
___ Exercise Bank	☐ Pupil's Edition p. 608
___ Create a Lesson Quiz	☐ 💿 Test Generator CD-ROM

Reteach

Using Support Materials	
___ Reteaching	☐ 📄 Grammar, Usage, and Mechanics Workbook p. 139

Homework Assignments

_____
_____
_____
_____
_____
_____
_____
_____

Other Teaching Materials

_____
_____
_____
_____
_____
_____
_____
_____
_____

CHAPTER 8

Lesson 6

Indefinite Pronouns as Antecedents

Pages 193–195

Lesson 6 Objectives
To recognize correct agreement with indefinite pronoun antecedents

To choose pronouns that agree with indefinite pronoun antecedents in sentences

Teach	Resources
Warm-Up	
___ Test Preparation	☐ 📖 Daily Test Prep. p. DT25
Using the Pupil's Edition	
___ Here's the Idea	☐ Pupil's Edition p. 193
___ Why It Matters in Writing	☐ Pupil's Edition p. 194

Practice and Apply

Using the Pupil's Edition	
___ Concept Check	☐ Pupil's Edition p. 195
___ Editing	☐ Pupil's Edition p. 195
Using Support Materials	
___ More Practice	☐ 🎞 Grammar, Usage, and Mechanics Workbook p. 143
___ Application	☐ 🎞 Grammar, Usage, and Mechanics Workbook p. 144
Using Technology	
___ Pronoun Antecedent Agreement I–II	☐ 💿 Grammar Coach CD-ROM, Lessons 7–8

Assess and Close

Ongoing Assessment Options	
___ Exercise Bank	☐ Pupil's Edition p. 608
___ Create a Lesson Quiz	☐ 💿 Test Generator CD-ROM

Reteach

Using Support Materials	
___ Reteaching	☐ 🎞 Grammar, Usage, and Mechanics Workbook p. 142

Homework Assignments

_____
_____
_____
_____
_____
_____
_____
_____

Other Teaching Materials

_____
_____
_____
_____
_____
_____
_____
_____
_____
_____

CHAPTER 8

Lesson 7

Pronoun Reference Problems

Pages 196–198

Lesson 7 Objectives
To identify pronoun reference problems
To rewrite sentences to correct faulty pronoun references

Teach	Resources
Warm-Up	
___ Test Preparation	☐ 🏛 Daily Test Prep. p. DT26
Using the Pupil's Edition	
___ Here's the Idea	☐ Pupil's Edition p. 196
___ Why It Matters in Writing	☐ Pupil's Edition p. 197
Using Support Materials	
___ Pronoun Reference Problems	☐ 🏛 Quick-Fix Grammar and Style Charts p. QF5

Practice and Apply

Using the Pupil's Edition	
___ Concept Check	☐ Pupil's Edition p. 198
___ Revising	☐ Pupil's Edition p. 198
Using Support Materials	
___ More Practice	☐ 📖 Grammar, Usage, and Mechanics Workbook p. 146
___ Application	☐ 📖 Grammar, Usage, and Mechanics Workbook p. 147
Using Technology	
___ Pronoun Antecedent Agreement II	☐ 💿 Grammar Coach CD-ROM, Lesson 8

Assess and Close

Ongoing Assessment Options	
___ Exercise Bank	☐ Pupil's Edition p. 609
___ Create a Lesson Quiz	☐ 💿 Test Generator CD-ROM

Reteach

Using Support Materials	
___ Reteaching	☐ 📖 Grammar, Usage, and Mechanics Workbook p. 145

Homework Assignments

_____
_____
_____
_____
_____
_____
_____
_____

Other Teaching Materials

_____
_____
_____
_____
_____
_____
_____
_____
_____

CHAPTER 8

Lesson 8

Other Pronoun Problems

Pages 199–201

Lesson 8 Objectives
To identify and choose the correct pronouns to use in appositives and comparisons

Teach	Resources
Warm-Up	
___ Test Preparation	☐ 🏛 Daily Test Prep. p. DT26
Using the Pupil's Edition	
___ Here's the Idea	☐ Pupil's Edition p. 199
___ Why It Matters in Writing	☐ Pupil's Edition p. 201

Practice and Apply

Using the Pupil's Edition	
___ Concept Check	☐ Pupil's Edition p. 201
___ Revising	☐ Pupil's Edition p. 201
Using Support Materials	
___ More Practice	☐ 🎞 Grammar, Usage, and Mechanics Workbook p. 149
___ Application	☐ 🎞 Grammar, Usage, and Mechanics Workbook p. 150
Using Technology	
___ Pronouns	☐ 💿 Grammar Coach CD-ROM, Lessons 7, 9

Assess and Close

Ongoing Assessment Options	
___ Exercise Bank	☐ Pupil's Edition p. 610
___ Create a Lesson Quiz	☐ 💿 Test Generator CD-ROM

Reteach

Using Support Materials	
___ Reteaching	☐ 🎞 Grammar, Usage, and Mechanics Workbook p. 148

Wrapping Up Chapter 8	Resources
Application and Review	
___ Real World Grammar	☐ Pupil's Edition pp. 202–203
___ Mixed Review	☐ Pupil's Edition p. 204
Assessment	
___ Mastery Test	☐ Pupil's Edition p. 205
___ Chapter Mastery Tests	☐ 🎞 Assessment Masters pp. 77–82 or 💿 Test Generator CD-ROM
___ Grammar Chapter Quiz	☐ 🐭 mcdougallittell.com

Homework Assignments

_____
_____
_____
_____
_____
_____
_____
_____
_____
_____

Other Teaching Materials

_____
_____
_____
_____
_____
_____
_____
_____
_____
_____

CHAPTER 8

CHAPTER 9

Preparing for Chapter 9

Resources

Warm-Up
___ Write Away

☐ Pupil's Edition p. 208

Diagnostic Testing
___ Diagnostic Test
___ Chapter Pretest

☐ Pupils' Edition p. 209
☐ 📖 Assessment Masters pp. 18–19 or
💿 Test Generator CD-ROM

Lesson 1 — Using Adjectives and Adverbs

Pages 210–212

Lesson 1 Objectives
To distinguish between adjectives and adverbs and to use them correctly in sentences

Teach

Resources

Warm-Up
___ Test Preparation

☐ 📘 Daily Test Prep. p. DT27

Using the Pupil's Edition
___ Here's the Idea
___ Why It Matters in Writing

☐ Pupil's Edition p. 210
☐ Pupil's Edition p. 211

Practice and Apply

Using the Pupil's Edition
___ Concept Check
___ Writing

☐ Pupil's Edition p. 212
☐ Pupil's Edition p. 212

Using Support Materials
___ More Practice

___ Application

☐ 📖 Grammar, Usage, and Mechanics Workbook p. 152
☐ 📖 Grammar, Usage, and Mechanics Workbook p. 153

Using Technology
___ Misplaced and Dangling Modifiers

☐ 💿 Grammar Coach CD-ROM, Lesson 12

Customizing the Lesson
___ Adjectives vs. Adverbs

☐ 🎧 SAE/ESL English Grammar Survival Kit pp. 11–12

Homework Assignments

_____
_____
_____
_____
_____
_____
_____
_____
_____
_____

Other Teaching Materials

_____
_____
_____
_____
_____
_____
_____
_____
_____
_____
_____
_____

Lesson 1

Using Adjectives and Adverbs (continued)

Pages 210–212

Assess and Close

Ongoing Assessment Options
___ Exercise Bank
___ Create a Lesson Quiz

Reteach

Using Support Materials
___ Reteaching

Resources

☐ Pupil's Edition p. 611
☐ ⊛ Test Generator CD-ROM

☐ ▦ Grammar, Usage, and
    Mechanics Workbook p. 151

Homework Assignments

_____
_____
_____
_____
_____
_____
_____
_____
_____

Other Teaching Materials

_____
_____
_____
_____
_____
_____
_____
_____
_____

Lesson 2

Problems with Modifiers

Pages 213–216

Lesson 2 Objectives
To identify and correct problems with modifiers in sentences

Teach	Resources
Warm-Up	
___ Test Preparation	☐ 🗄 Daily Test Prep. p. DT27
Using the Pupil's Edition	
___ Here's the Idea	☐ Pupil's Edition p. 213
___ Why It Matters in Writing	☐ Pupil's Edition p. 215

Practice and Apply

Using the Pupil's Edition	
___ Concept Check	☐ Pupil's Edition p. 216
___ Editing and Proofreading	☐ Pupil's Edition p. 216
___ Writing	☐ Pupil's Edition p. 216
Using Support Materials	
___ More Practice	☐ 📖 Grammar, Usage, and Mechanics Workbook p. 155
___ Application	☐ 📖 Grammar, Usage, and Mechanics Workbook p. 156
Customizing the Lesson	
___ Verbs: Negative Constructions	☐ 🎧 SAE/ESL English Grammar Survival Kit pp. 41–42

Assess and Close

Ongoing Assessment Options	
___ Chapter Mid-point Test	☐ 📖 Assessment Masters p. 32
___ Exercise Bank	☐ Pupil's Edition p. 611
___ Create a Lesson Quiz	☐ 💿 Test Generator CD-ROM

Reteach

Using Support Materials	
___ Reteaching	☐ 📖 Grammar, Usage, and Mechanics Workbook p. 154

Homework Assignments
_____
_____
_____
_____
_____
_____
_____
_____
_____

Other Teaching Materials
_____
_____
_____
_____
_____
_____
_____
_____
_____
_____

Lesson 3

Using Comparisons

Pages 217–219

Lesson 3 Objectives

To identify regular and irregular comparative forms and to use them correctly

Teach

Warm-Up
___ Test Preparation

Using the Pupil's Edition
___ Here's the Idea
___ Why It Matters in Writing

Using Support Materials
___ Confusing Comparisons

Practice and Apply

Using the Pupil's Edition
___ Concept Check
___ Writing

Using Support Materials
___ More Practice

___ Application

Using Technology
___ Confusing Comparisons

Assess and Close

Ongoing Assessment Options
___ Exercise Bank
___ Create a Lesson Quiz

Reteach

Using Support Materials
___ Reteaching

Resources

☐ 🏛 Daily Test Prep. p. DT28

☐ Pupil's Edition p. 217
☐ Pupil's Edition p. 218

☐ 🏛 Quick-Fix Grammar and Style Charts p. QF8

☐ Pupil's Edition p. 219
☐ Pupil's Edition p. 219

☐ 🎞 Grammar, Usage, and Mechanics Workbook p. 158
☐ 🎞 Grammar, Usage, and Mechanics Workbook p. 159

☐ 💿 Grammar Coach CD-ROM, Lesson 11

☐ Pupil's Edition p. 612
☐ 💿 Test Generator CD-ROM

☐ 🎞 Grammar, Usage, and Mechanics Workbook p. 157

Homework Assignments

_____
_____
_____
_____
_____
_____
_____
_____
_____

Other Teaching Materials

_____
_____
_____
_____
_____
_____
_____
_____
_____
_____

Lesson 4

Problems with Comparisons

Pages 220–221

Lesson 4 Objectives
To identify double comparisons and illogical comparisons and to correct them in sentences

Teach

	Resources

Warm-Up
___ Test Preparation

☐ 📖 Daily Test Prep. p. DT28

Using the Pupil's Edition
___ Here's the Idea
___ Why It Matters in Writing

☐ Pupil's Edition p. 220
☐ Pupil's Edition p. 221

Using Support Materials
___ Confusing Comparisons

☐ 📖 Quick-Fix Grammar and Style Charts p. QF8

Practice and Apply

Using the Pupil's Edition
___ Concept Check

☐ Pupil's Edition p. 221

Using Support Materials
___ More Practice

☐ 📖 Grammar, Usage, and Mechanics Workbook p. 161

___ Application

☐ 📖 Grammar, Usage, and Mechanics Workbook p. 162

Using Technology
___ Confusing Comparisons

☐ 💿 Grammar Coach CD-ROM, Lesson 11

Assess and Close

Ongoing Assessment Options
___ Exercise Bank
___ Create a Lesson Quiz

☐ Pupil's Edition p. 612
☐ 💿 Test Generator CD-ROM

Reteach

Using Support Materials
___ Reteaching

☐ 📖 Grammar, Usage, and Mechanics Workbook p. 160

Homework Assignments

_____
_____
_____
_____
_____
_____
_____
_____
_____

Other Teaching Materials

_____
_____
_____
_____
_____
_____
_____
_____
_____

Lesson 4

Problems with Comparisons *(continued)*

Pages 220–221

Wrapping Up Chapter 8

Application and Review
___ Real World Grammar
___ Mixed Review

Assessment
___ Mastery Test
___ Chapter Mastery Tests

___ Grammar Chapter Quiz

Resources

☐ Pupil's Edition pp. 222–223
☐ Pupil's Edition p. 224

☐ Pupil's Edition p. 225
☐ 📓 Assessment Masters
    pp. 83–86 or
    💿 Test Generator CD-ROM
☐ 🖥 mcdougallittell.com

Homework Assignments

_____
_____
_____
_____
_____
_____
_____
_____
_____
_____

Other Teaching Materials

_____
_____
_____
_____
_____
_____
_____
_____
_____
_____

Preparing for Chapter 10 | Resources

Warm-Up
___ Write Away

☐ Pupil's Edition p. 228

Diagnostic Testing
___ Diagnostic Test
___ Chapter Pretest

☐ Pupils' Edition p. 229
☐ 📠 Assessment Masters
    pp. 20–21 or
    💿 Test Generator CD-ROM

Lesson 1 — People and Cultures

Pages 230–232

Lesson 1 Objectives

To understand the rules for capitalizing the names of people and cultures and to use these rules to correct capitalization errors

Teach | Resources

Warm-Up
___ Test Preparation

☐ 🏛 Daily Test Prep. p. DT29

Using the Pupil's Edition
___ Here's the Idea

☐ Pupil's Edition p. 230

Practice and Apply

Using the Pupil's Edition
___ Concept Check
___ Revision

☐ Pupil's Edition p. 232
☐ Pupil's Edition p. 232

Using Support Materials
___ More Practice

___ Application

☐ 📠 Grammar, Usage, and
    Mechanics Workbook p. 164
☐ 📠 Grammar, Usage, and
    Mechanics Workbook p. 165

Assess and Close

Ongoing Assessment Options
___ Exercise Bank
___ Create a Lesson Quiz

☐ Pupil's Edition p. 613
☐ 💿 Test Generator CD-ROM

Reteach

Using Support Materials
___ Reteaching

☐ 📠 Grammar, Usage, and
    Mechanics Workbook p. 163

Homework Assignments
_____
_____
_____
_____
_____
_____
_____
_____
_____
_____

Other Teaching Materials
_____
_____
_____
_____
_____
_____
_____
_____
_____
_____

Lesson 2

First Words and Titles

Pages 233–235

Lesson 2 Objectives
To understand the rules for capitalizing first words and titles and to use these rules to correct errors in capitalization

Teach	**Resources**
Warm-Up	
___ Test Preparation	☐ 🏛 Daily Test Prep. p. DT29
Using the Pupil's Edition	
___ Here's the Idea	☐ Pupil's Edition p. 233

Practice and Apply

Using the Pupil's Edition	
___ Concept Check	☐ Pupil's Edition p. 235
___ Editing and Proofreading	☐ Pupil's Edition p. 235
Using Support Materials	
___ More Practice	☐ 🎞 Grammar, Usage, and Mechanics Workbook p. 167
___ Application	☐ 🎞 Grammar, Usage, and Mechanics Workbook p. 168

Assess and Close

Ongoing Assessment Options	
___ Chapter Mid-point Test	☐ 🎞 Assessment Masters p. 33
___ Exercise Bank	☐ Pupil's Edition p. 614
___ Create a Lesson Quiz	☐ 💿 Test Generator CD-ROM

Reteach

Using Support Materials	
___ Reteaching	☐ 🎞 Grammar, Usage, and Mechanics Workbook p. 166

Homework Assignments

_____
_____
_____
_____
_____
_____
_____
_____
_____

Other Teaching Materials

_____
_____
_____
_____
_____
_____
_____
_____
_____
_____

Lesson 3

Places and Transportation

Pages 236–238

Lesson 3 Objectives
To understand the rules for capitalizing names of particular places, planets, landmarks and vehicles and to use these rules to correct capitalization errors

CHAPTER 10

Teach

	Resources
Warm-Up	
___ Test Preparation	☐ 📖 Daily Test Prep. p. DT30
Using the Pupil's Edition	
___ Here's the Idea	☐ Pupil's Edition p.236

Practice and Apply

Using the Pupil's Edition	
___ Concept Check	☐ Pupil's Edition p. 238
___ Editing and Proofreading	☐ Pupil's Edition p. 238
Using Support Materials	
___ More Practice	☐ 📖 Grammar, Usage, and Mechanics Workbook p. 170
___ Application	☐ 📖 Grammar, Usage, and Mechanics Workbook p. 171

Assess and Close

Ongoing Assessment Options	
___ Exercise Bank	☐ Pupil's Edition p. 615
___ Create a Lesson Quiz	☐ 💿 Test Generator CD-ROM

Reteach

Using Support Materials	
___ Reteaching	☐ 📖 Grammar, Usage, and Mechanics Workbook p. 169

Homework Assignments

_____
_____
_____
_____
_____
_____
_____
_____
_____

Other Teaching Materials

_____
_____
_____
_____
_____
_____
_____
_____
_____

Lesson 4

Organizations and Other Subjects

Pages 239–241

Lesson 4 Objectives
To understand the rules for capitalizing names of organizations, acronyms, names of historical events, and various words and abbreviations
To use these rules to correct capitalization errors

Teach	Resources
Warm-Up	
___ Test Preparation	☐ 🏛 Daily Test Prep. p. DT30
Using the Pupil's Edition	
___ Here's the Idea	☐ Pupil's Edition p. 239

Practice and Apply

Using the Pupil's Edition	
___ Concept Check	☐ Pupil's Edition p. 241
___ Mixed Review	☐ Pupil's Edition p. 241
Using Support Materials	
___ More Practice	☐ 📖 Grammar, Usage, and Mechanics Workbook p. 173
___ Application	☐ 📖 Grammar, Usage, and Mechanics Workbook p. 174

Assess and Close

Ongoing Assessment Options	
___ Exercise Bank	☐ Pupil's Edition p. 615
___ Create a Lesson Quiz	☐ 💿 Test Generator CD-ROM

Reteach

Using Support Materials	
___ Reteaching	☐ 📖 Grammar, Usage, and Mechanics Workbook p. 172

Homework Assignments

_____
_____
_____
_____
_____
_____
_____
_____
_____

Wrapping Up Chapter 10	Resources
Application and Review	
___ Real World Grammar	☐ Pupil's Edition pp. 242–243
___ Mixed Review	☐ Pupil's Edition p. 244
Assessment	
___ Mastery Test	☐ Pupil's Edition p. 245
___ Chapter Mastery Tests	☐ 📖 Assessment Masters pp. 87–90 or 💿 Test Generator CD-ROM
___ Grammar Chapter Quiz	☐ 🌐 mcdougallittell.com

Other Teaching Materials

_____
_____
_____
_____
_____
_____
_____
_____
_____

Preparing for Chapter 11 — Resources

Warm-Up
___ Write Away
☐ Pupil's Edition p. 248

Diagnostic Testing
___ Diagnostic Test
___ Chapter Pretest
☐ Pupils' Edition p. 249
☐ 📰 Assessment Masters
    pp. 22–23 or
    💿 Test Generator CD-ROM

Lesson 1 — Periods and Other End Marks

Pages 250–251

Lesson 1 Objectives
To recognize periods, question marks, and exclamation points as end marks and to use them in writing

Teach	Resources

Warm-Up
___ Test Preparation
☐ 🏛 Daily Test Prep. p. DT31

Using the Pupil's Edition
___ Here's the Idea
☐ Pupil's Edition p. 250

Practice and Apply

Using the Pupil's Edition
___ Concept Check
☐ Pupil's Edition p. 251

Using Support Materials
___ More Practice
☐ 📰 Grammar, Usage, and Mechanics Workbook p. 176

___ Application
☐ 📰 Grammar, Usage, and Mechanics Workbook p. 177

Assess and Close

Ongoing Assessment Options
___ Exercise Bank
___ Create a Lesson Quiz
☐ Pupil's Edition p. 616
☐ 💿 Test Generator CD-ROM

Reteach

Using Support Materials
___ Reteaching
☐ 📰 Grammar, Usage, and Mechanics Workbook p. 175

Homework Assignments
_____
_____
_____
_____
_____
_____
_____
_____
_____
_____

Other Teaching Materials
_____
_____
_____
_____
_____
_____
_____
_____
_____

Lesson 2

Commas in Sentence Parts

Pages 252–254

Lesson 2 Objectives
To recognize that commas are used in a series, following
introductory elements, and with interrupters, and to use commas
in sentence parts

Teach	**Resources**
Warm-Up ___ Test Preparation	☐ 🏛 Daily Test Prep. p. DT31
Using the Pupil's Edition ___ Here's the Idea	☐ Pupil's Edition p. 252
Using Support Materials ___ Missing or Misplaced Commas	☐ 🏛 Quick-Fix Grammar and Style Charts p. QF11

Practice and Apply

Using the Pupil's Edition ___ Concept Check	☐ Pupil's Edition p. 254
Using Support Materials ___ More Practice	☐ 📖 Grammar, Usage, and Mechanics Workbook p. 179
___ Application	☐ 📖 Grammar, Usage, and Mechanics Workbook p. 180
Using Technology ___ Comma Mistakes	☐ 💿 Grammar Coach CD-ROM, Lesson 3

Assess and Close

Ongoing Assessment Options ___ Exercise Bank ___ Create a Lesson Quiz	☐ Pupil's Edition p. 617 ☐ 💿 Test Generator CD-ROM

Reteach

Using Support Materials ___ Reteaching	☐ 📖 Grammar, Usage, and Mechanics Workbook p. 178

CHAPTER 11

Homework Assignments
_____
_____
_____
_____
_____
_____
_____
_____
_____

Other Teaching Materials
_____
_____
_____
_____
_____
_____
_____
_____
_____
_____

Lesson 3

More Commas

Lesson 3 Objectives
To understand the various uses of commas, to recognize the need for commas, and to use these in sentences

Teach

Teach	Resources

Warm-Up
___ Test Preparation
☐ 🏛 Daily Test Prep. p. DT32

Using the Pupil's Edition
___ Here's the Idea
☐ Pupil's Edition p. 255

Using Support Materials
___ Missing or Misplaced Commas
☐ 🏛 Quick-Fix Grammar and Style Charts p. QF11

Practice and Apply

Using the Pupil's Edition
___ Concept Check
☐ Pupil's Edition p. 257
___ Proofreading
☐ Pupil's Edition p. 257

Using Support Materials
___ More Practice
☐ 🎞 Grammar, Usage, and Mechanics Workbook p. 182

___ Application
☐ 🎞 Grammar, Usage, and Mechanics Workbook p. 183

Using Technology
___ [???Grammar Coach Lesson Name???]
☐ 💿 Grammar Coach CD-ROM, Lessons 2–3

Assess and Close

Ongoing Assessment Options
___ Exercise Bank
☐ Pupil's Edition p. 617
___ Create a Lesson Quiz
☐ 💿 Test Generator CD-ROM

Reteach

Using Support Materials
___ Reteaching
☐ 🎞 Grammar, Usage, and Mechanics Workbook p. 181

Homework Assignments
_____
_____
_____
_____
_____
_____
_____
_____

Other Teaching Materials
_____
_____
_____
_____
_____
_____
_____
_____

Lesson 4 **Semicolons and Colons**   *Pages 258–259*

Lesson 4 Objectives
To recognize the role of semicolons and colons and to use colons and semicolons in sentences

Teach	Resources
Warm-Up	
___ Test Preparation	☐ ▦ Daily Test Prep. p. DT32
Using the Pupil's Edition	
___ Here's the Idea	☐ Pupil's Edition p. 258

Practice and Apply

Using the Pupil's Edition	
___ Concept Check	☐ Pupil's Edition p. 259
Using Support Materials	
___ More Practice	☐ ▦ Grammar, Usage, and Mechanics Workbook p. 185
___ Application	☐ ▦ Grammar, Usage, and Mechanics Workbook p. 186

Assess and Close

Ongoing Assessment Options	
___ Chapter Mid-point Test	☐ ▦ Assessment Masters p. 34
___ Exercise Bank	☐ Pupil's Edition p. 618
___ Create a Lesson Quiz	☐ ◉ Test Generator CD-ROM

Reteach

Using Support Materials	
___ Reteaching	☐ ▦ Grammar, Usage, and Mechanics Workbook p. 184

Homework Assignments

_____
_____
_____
_____
_____
_____
_____
_____

Other Teaching Materials

_____
_____
_____
_____
_____
_____
_____
_____

Lesson 5

Quotation Marks

Pages 260–263

Lesson 5 Objectives
To recognize the uses for quotation marks and to use quotation marks in writing

THE LANGUAGE OF LITERATURE Connect to *The Bass, the River, and Sheila Mant,* Level 9.

Teach	Resources
Warm-Up	
___ Test Preparation	☐ 🏛 Daily Test Prep. p. DT33
Using the Pupil's Edition	
___ Here's the Idea	☐ Pupil's Edition p. 260

Practice and Apply

Using the Pupil's Edition	
___ Concept Check	☐ Pupil's Edition p. 262
___ Proofreading	☐ Pupil's Edition p. 263
Using Support Materials	
___ More Practice	☐ 📖 Grammar, Usage, and Mechanics Workbook p. 188
___ Application	☐ 📖 Grammar, Usage, and Mechanics Workbook p. 189
Using Technology	
___ Comma Mistakes	☐ 💿 Grammar Coach CD-ROM, Lesson 3

Assess and Close

Ongoing Assessment Options	
___ Exercise Bank	☐ Pupil's Edition p. 619
___ Create a Lesson Quiz	☐ 💿 Test Generator CD-ROM

Reteach

Using Support Materials	
___ Reteaching	☐ 📖 Grammar, Usage, and Mechanics Workbook p. 187

Homework Assignments

_____
_____
_____
_____
_____
_____
_____
_____
_____

Other Teaching Materials

_____
_____
_____
_____
_____
_____
_____
_____
_____

Lesson 6

Other Punctuation

Pages 264–267

Lesson 6 Objectives
To recognize the uses for hyphens, apostrophes, dashes, and parentheses, and to use these marks in writing

Teach

	Resources

Warm-Up
___ Test Preparation

☐ 🏛 Daily Test Prep. p. DT33

Using the Pupil's Edition
___ Here's the Idea

☐ Pupil's Edition p. 264

Practice and Apply

Using the Pupil's Edition
___ Concept Check

☐ Pupil's Edition p. 267

Using Support Materials
___ More Practice

☐ 📓 Grammar, Usage, and Mechanics Workbook p. 191

___ Application

☐ 📓 Grammar, Usage, and Mechanics Workbook p. 192

Assess and Close

Ongoing Assessment Options
___ Exercise Bank
___ Create a Lesson Quiz

☐ Pupil's Edition p. 620
☐ 💿 Test Generator CD-ROM

Reteach

Using Support Materials
___ Reteaching

☐ 📓 Grammar, Usage, and Mechanics Workbook p. 190

CHAP

Homework Assignments

_____
_____
_____
_____
_____
_____
_____
_____

Other Teaching Materials

_____
_____
_____
_____
_____
_____
_____
_____
_____

Lesson 7

Ellipses and Italics

Pages 268–269

Lesson 7 Objectives
To recognize the uses for ellipses and italics and to use ellipses and italics in writing

Teach | Resources

Warm-Up
___ Test Preparation   ☐ 🏛 Daily Test Prep. p. DT34

Using the Pupil's Edition
___ Here's the Idea   ☐ Pupil's Edition p. 268

Practice and Apply

Using the Pupil's Edition
___ Concept Check   ☐ Pupil's Edition p. 269
___ Revising   ☐ Pupil's Edition p. 269

Using Support Materials
___ More Practice   ☐ 📖 Grammar, Usage, and
                               Mechanics Workbook p. 194
___ Application   ☐ 📖 Grammar, Usage, and
                               Mechanics Workbook p. 195

Assess and Close

Ongoing Assessment Options
___ Exercise Bank   ☐ Pupil's Edition p. 621
___ Create a Lesson Quiz   ☐ 💿 Test Generator CD-ROM

Reteach

Using Support Materials
___ Reteaching   ☐ 📖 Grammar, Usage, and
                              Mechanics Workbook p. 193

Wrapping Up Chapter 11 | Resources

Application and Review
___ Real World Grammar   ☐ Pupil's Edition pp. 270–271
___ Mixed Review   ☐ Pupil's Edition p. 272

Assessment
___ Mastery Test   ☐ Pupil's Edition p. 273
___ Chapter Mastery Tests   ☐ 📖 Assessment Masters
                               pp. 91–96 or
                               💿 Test Generator CD-ROM
___ Grammar Chapter Quiz   ☐ 💿 mcdougallittell.com

Homework Assignments

_____
_____
_____
_____
_____
_____
_____
_____
_____

Other Teaching Materials

_____
_____
_____
_____
_____
_____
_____
_____
_____

Preparing for Chapter 12   Resources

Warm-Up
___ Power Words
___ Write Away

☐ Pupil's Edition p. 302
☐ Pupil's Edition p. 303

Lesson 1 — Prewriting

Pages 304–306

Lesson 1 Objectives
To recognize prewriting as the first step in the writing process and to identify a variety or prewriting techniques

Teach   Resources

Warm-Up
___ Test Preparation

☐ 🏛 Daily Test Prep. p. DT34

Using the Pupil's Edition
___ Asking Questions
___ Exploring a Topic
___ Refining a Topic
___ Gathering and Organizing Ideas

☐ Pupil's Edition p. 304
☐ Pupil's Edition p. 305
☐ Pupil's Edition p. 306
☐ Pupil's Edition p. 306

Using Support Materials
___ Cluster Diagram, Spider Map, Venn Diagram, Sequence Chain
___ Writing Variables

☐ 🏛 Critical Thinking Graphic Organizers pp. CT3, 5, 7, 9

☐ 🏛 Writing and Communication Skills p. WC1

Practice and Apply

Using Support Materials
___ Asking Questions

___ Writing Process

☐ 📰 Writing and Communication Masters p. 1
☐ 📰 SAE/ESL side by Side p. 17

Assess and Close

Ongoing Assessment Options
___ Assessment Information

☐ 📰 Teacher's Guide to Assessment and Portfolio Use

Homework Assignments
_____
_____
_____
_____
_____
_____
_____
_____
_____

Other Teaching Materials
_____
_____
_____
_____
_____
_____
_____
_____
_____
_____
_____

CHAPTER 12

Lesson 2

Drafting

Lesson 2 Objectives

To recognize drafting as a step in the writing process and to become familiar with the steps in preparing a draft

Teach	Resources
Warm-Up	
___ Test Preparation	☐ 📖 Daily Test Prep. p. DT35
Using the Pupil's Edition	
___ Drafting to Discover	☐ Pupil's Edition p. 307
___ Drafting from a Plan	☐ Pupil's Edition p. 307
___ Using Peer Response	☐ Pupil's Edition p. 308

Practice and Apply

Using Support Materials	
___ Using Peer Response	☐ 📖 Writing and Communication Masters p. 2

Assess and Close

Ongoing Assessment Options	
___ Assessment Information	☐ 📖 Teacher's Guide to Assessment and Portfolio Use

---

Homework Assignments

_____
_____
_____
_____
_____
_____
_____
_____
_____
_____

Other Teaching Materials

_____
_____
_____
_____
_____
_____
_____
_____
_____
_____

Lesson 3 **Revising**

Lesson 3 Objectives
To identify and use the traits of effective writing

THE LANGUAGE OF
LITERATURE Connect to *The Cask of Amontillado,* Level 9.

Teach	Resources
Warm-Up	
___ Test Preparation	☐ 🏛 Daily Test Prep. p. DT35
Using the Pupil's Edition	
___ Six Traits of Effective Writing	☐ Pupil's Edition p. 309
Using Support Materials	
___ Evaluation Traits	☐ 🏛 Writing and Communication Skills p. WC2

Practice and Apply

Using Support Materials	
___ Revising	☐ ▤ Writing and Communication Masters p. 3

Assess and Close

Ongoing Assessment Options	
___ Assessment Information	☐ ▤ Teacher's Guide to Assessment and Portfolio Use

CHAPTER 12

Homework Assignments
_____
_____
_____
_____
_____
_____
_____
_____
_____

Other Teaching Materials
_____
_____
_____
_____
_____
_____
_____
_____
_____

Lesson 4

Editing and Proofreading

Pages 312–313

Lesson 4 Objectives
To recognize editing and proofreading as steps in the writing process
To use editing and proofreading techniques, including proofreading marks

Teach	Resources
Warm-Up ___ Test Preparation	☐ 🖥 Daily Test Prep. p. DT36
Using the Pupil's Edition ___ Editing and Proofreading Techniques ___ Using Proofreading Marks	☐ Pupil's Edition p. 312 ☐ Pupil's Edition p. 313
Using Support Materials ___ Proofreading Marks	☐ 🏛 Writing and Communication Skills p. WC3

Practice and Apply

Using Support Materials ___ Editing and Proofreading	☐ 🖼 Writing and Communication Masters p. 4

Assess and Close

Ongoing Assessment Options ___ Assessment Information	☐ 🖼 Teacher's Guide to Assessment and Portfolio Use

CHAPTER 12

Homework Assignments

_____
_____
_____
_____
_____
_____
_____
_____
_____
_____
_____
_____

Other Teaching Materials

_____
_____
_____
_____
_____
_____
_____
_____
_____
_____
_____
_____

Lesson 5 — Publishing and Reflecting

Pages 314–315

Lesson 5 Objectives
To recognize ways to publish written work and to reflect on the writing process

Teach	Resources

Warm-Up
___ Test Preparation

☐ 🏛 Daily Test Prep. p. DT36

Using the Pupil's Edition
___ Sharing Your Writing
___ Reflecting on Your Writing

☐ Pupil's Edition p. 314
☐ Pupil's Edition p. 315

Practice and Apply

Using Support Materials
___ Sharing Your Writing

☐ 📖 Writing and Communication Masters p. 5

Assess and Close

Ongoing Assessment Options
___ Assessment Information

☐ 📖 Teacher's Guide to Assessment and Portfolio Use

CHAPTER 12

Homework Assignments
_____
_____
_____
_____
_____
_____
_____
_____
_____

Other Teaching Materials
_____
_____
_____
_____
_____
_____
_____
_____
_____

Preparing for Chapter 13 | Resources

Warm-Up
___ Power Words
___ Write Away

☐ Pupil's Edition p. 318
☐ Pupil's Edition p. 319

Building Effective Sentences

Pages 320–321

Lesson 1 Objectives
To recognize characteristics of effective sentences and to use these characteristics as guidelines in revising sentences

Teach | Resources

Warm-Up
___ Test Preparation

☐ 🏛 Daily Test Prep. p. DT37

Using the Pupil's Edition
___ Expressing Thoughts Effectively

☐ Pupil's Edition p. 320

___ Making Your Words Picture Perfect

☐ Pupil's Edition p. 320

___ Cutting Out the Fluff

☐ Pupil's Edition p. 321

Using Support Materials
___ Improving Style

☐ 🏛 Quick-Fix Grammar and Style Charts pp. QF13–14

___ Sensory Word List

☐ 🏛 Writing and Communication Skills p. WC9

Practice and Apply

Using the Pupil's Edition
___ Practice

☐ Pupil's Edition p. 321

Using Support Materials
___ Cutting Out the Fluff

☐ 🖥 Writing and Communication Masters p. 6

Assess and Close

Ongoing Assessment Options
___ Assessment Information

☐ 🖥 Teacher's Guide to Assessment and Portfolio Use

Homework Assignments
_____
_____
_____
_____
_____
_____
_____
_____
_____
_____
_____
_____

Other Teaching Materials
_____
_____
_____
_____
_____
_____
_____
_____
_____
_____
_____

CHAPTER 13

Writing Effective Paragraphs

Lesson 2

Pages 322–325

Lesson 2 Objectives
To recognize the characteristics of the four main types of paragraphs and to practice writing each type of paragraph

 THE LANGUAGE OF LITERATURE Connect to *Marigolds, Two Kinds,* Level 9.

Teach	Resources
Warm-Up	
___ Test Preparation	☐ 🏛 Daily Test Prep. p. DT37
Using the Pupil's Edition	
___ What is a Paragraph?	☐ Pupil's Edition p. 322
___ Descriptive Paragraphs	☐ Pupil's Edition p. 322
___ Narrative Paragraphs	☐ Pupil's Edition p. 323
___ Informative Paragraphs	☐ Pupil's Edition p. 324
___ Persuasive Paragraphs	☐ Pupil's Edition p. 325
Using Support Materials	
___ Paragraphing 1–2	☐ 🏛 Quick-Fix Grammar and Style Charts p. QF21–22

Practice and Apply

Using the Pupil's Edition	
___ Practice A	☐ Pupil's Edition p. 323
___ Practice B	☐ Pupil's Edition p. 323
___ Practice C	☐ Pupil's Edition p. 324
___ Practice D	☐ Pupil's Edition p. 325
Using Support Materials	
___ Paragraph Unity	☐ 📖 Writing and Communication Masters p. 7

Assess and Close

Ongoing Assessment Options	
___ Assessment Information	☐ 📖 Teacher's Guide to Assessment and Portfolio Use

Homework Assignments

_____
_____
_____
_____
_____
_____
_____
_____
_____

Other Teaching Materials

_____
_____
_____
_____
_____
_____
_____
_____

CHAPTER 13

CHAPTER 13

Lesson 3

Paragraph Unity

Pages 326–327

Lesson 3 Objectives
To recognize unity in a paragraph and to revise paragraphs for unity

THE LANGUAGE OF
LITERATURE   Connect to *Roll of Thunder Hear My Cry,* Level 9.

Teach	Resources
Warm-Up	
___ Test Preparation	☐ 📖 Daily Test Prep. p. DT38
Using the Pupil's Edition	
___ Understanding Unity	☐ Pupil's Edition p. 326
___ Topic Sentence	☐ Pupil's Edition p. 326
___ Implied Topic Sentence	☐ Pupil's Edition p. 327
Using Support Materials	
___ Topic Sentences	☐ 📖 Writing and Communication Skills p. WC6

Practice and Apply

Using the Pupil's Edition	
___ Practice	☐ Pupil's Edition p. 327
Using Support Materials	
___ Topic Sentences	☐ 📄 Writing and Communication Masters p. 8

Assess and Close

Ongoing Assessment Options	
___ Assessment Information	☐ 📄 Teacher's Guide to Assessment and Portfolio Use

Homework Assignments
_____
_____
_____
_____
_____
_____
_____
_____

Other Teaching Materials
_____
_____
_____
_____
_____
_____
_____
_____
_____

Lesson 4

Coherence

Pages 328–331

Lesson 4 Objectives

To recognize paragraph coherence and the five types of paragraph organization

To choose appropriate patterns of organization for various paragraph topics

 Connect to *Through the Tunnel, All Gold Canyon, I Know Why the Caged Bird Sings, The House on Mango Street,* Level 9.

Teach	**Resources**
Warm-Up	
___ Test Preparation	☐ 🖥 Daily Test Prep. p. DT38
Using the Pupil's Edition	
___ Sequential Order	☐ Pupil's Edition p. 328
___ Spatial Order	☐ Pupil's Edition p. 328
___ Cause and Effect	☐ Pupil's Edition p. 329
___ Comparison and Contrast	☐ Pupil's Edition p. 330
___ Order of Degree	☐ Pupil's Edition p. 331

Practice and Apply

Using the Pupil's Edition	
___ Practice	☐ Pupil's Edition p. 331
Customizing the Lesson	
___ Organizing Paragraphs	☐ 📖 SAE/ESL Side by Side pp. 18–20

Assess and Close

Ongoing Assessment Options	
___ Assessment Information	☐ 📖 Teacher's Guide to Assessment and Portfolio Use

Homework Assignments

_____
_____
_____
_____
_____
_____
_____
_____
_____

Other Teaching Materials

_____
_____
_____
_____
_____
_____
_____
_____
_____

CHAPTER 13

Preparing for Chapter 14

Warm-Up
___ Power Words
___ Write Away

Chapter Resources
___ Developing Compositions

Resources

☐ Pupil's Edition p. 334
☐ Pupil's Edition p. 335

☐ ⊛ Power Presentations
   CD-ROM Lesson 7

Lesson 1

What Is a Composition?

Pages 336–337

Lesson 1 Objectives
To recognize the three parts of a composition and to identify them in a writing sample

Teach

Warm-Up
___ Test Preparation

Using the Pupil's Edition
___ What's the Idea?

Using Support Materials
___ Organizing an Expository
   Composition

Practice and Apply

Customizing the Lesson
___ Five-Paragraph

Assess and Close

Ongoing Assessment Options
___ Assessment Information

Resources

☐ 📕 Daily Test Prep. p. DT39

☐ Pupil's Edition p. 336

☐ 📕 Writing and Communication
   Skills p. WC5

☐ 📰 SAE/ESL Side by Side p. 21

☐ 📰 Teacher's Guide to Assessment and Portfolio Use

Homework Assignments
_____
_____
_____
_____
_____
_____
_____
_____

Other Teaching Materials
_____
_____
_____
_____
_____
_____
_____
_____

CHAPTER 14

Lesson 2

Creating a Thesis Statement

Pages 338–339

Lesson 2 Objectives

To recognize the purpose of a thesis statement, to identify properly focused thesis statements, and to revise thesis statements in an appropriate manner

Teach

Resources

Warm-Up
___ Test Preparation

☐ 📖 Daily Test Prep. p. DT39

Using the Pupil's Edition
___ Writing a Thesis Statement

☐ Pupil's Edition p. 338

Using Support Materials
___ Thesis Statement

☐ 📖 Writing and Communication
    Skills p. WC7

Practice and Apply

Using the Pupil's Edition
___ Practice

☐ Pupil's Edition p. 339

Using Support Materials
___ Crafting a Thesis
    Statement

☐ 📖 Writing and Communication
    Masters p. 11

Assess and Close

Ongoing Assessment Options
___ Assessment Information

☐ 📖 Teacher's Guide to Assess-
    ment and Portfolio Use

Homework Assignments

_____
_____
_____
_____
_____
_____
_____
_____
_____
_____
_____

Other Teaching Materials

_____
_____
_____
_____
_____
_____
_____
_____
_____
_____

CHAPTER 14

Lesson 3

Effective Introductions

Pages 340–341

Lesson 3 Objectives
To recognize the purpose of an introduction, to understand various ways of engaging readers' attention, and to apply this information in writing

Teach

Resources

Warm-Up
___ Test Preparation

☐ 🏛 Daily Test Prep. p. DT40

Using the Pupil's Edition
___ Engaging the Reader

☐ Pupil's Edition p. 340

Practice and Apply

Using the Pupil's Edition
___ Practice

☐ Pupil's Edition p. 341

Using Support Materials
___ Effective Introductions

☐ 📰 Writing and Communication Masters p. 12

Assess and Close

Ongoing Assessment Options
___ Assessment Information

☐ 📰 Teacher's Guide to Assessment and Portfolio Use

Homework Assignments

_____
_____
_____
_____
_____
_____
_____
_____
_____
_____
_____

Other Teaching Materials

_____
_____
_____
_____
_____
_____
_____
_____
_____
_____
_____

CHAPTER 14

Copyright © McDougal Littell Inc.

Lesson 4

Body: Unity

Pages 342–343

Lesson 4 Objectives
To understand how to achieve unity in a composition
To recognize sentences that do not support a thesis statement

Teach

Warm-Up
___ Test Preparation

Using the Pupil's Edition
___ Achieving Unity
___ Creating Topic Sentences
___ Paragraphing

Using Support Materials
___ Cluster Diagrams, Spider Map, Venn Diagram
___ Topic Sentences

Practice and Apply

Using the Pupil's Edition
___ Practice

Using Support Materials
___ Unity in Compositions

Assess and Close

Ongoing Assessment Options
___ Assessment Information

Resources

☐ 🏛 Daily Test Prep. p. DT40

☐ Pupil's Edition p. 342
☐ Pupil's Edition p. 343
☐ Pupil's Edition p. 343

☐ 🏛 Critical Thinking Graphic Organizers p. CT3, 5, 7
☐ 🏛 Writing and Communication Skills p. WC6

☐ Pupil's Edition p. 343

☐ 🖽 Writing and Communication Masters p. 13

☐ 🖽 Teacher's Guide to Assessment and Portfolio Use

Homework Assignments

_____
_____
_____
_____
_____
_____

Other Teaching Materials

_____
_____
_____
_____
_____
_____
_____
_____

CHAPTER 14

Lesson 5

Body: Coherence

Pages 344–345

Lesson 5 Objectives
To determine whether a composition is coherent and to understand various ways of achieving coherence

Teach	**Resources**
Warm-Up	
___ Test Preparation	☐ 📖 Daily Test Prep. p. DT41
Using the Pupil's Edition	
___ Achieving Coherence	☐ Pupil's Edition p. 344
Using Support Materials	
___ Transitional Words	☐ 🏛 Writing and Communication Skills p. WC4
Practice and Apply	
Using the Pupil's Edition	
___ Practice	☐ Pupil's Edition p. 345
Using Support Materials	
___ Using Transitional Devices	☐ 📖 Writing and Communication Masters p. 14
Assess and Close	
Ongoing Assessment Options	
___ Assessment Information	☐ 📖 Teacher's Guide to Assessment and Portfolio Use

Homework Assignments

_____
_____
_____
_____
_____
_____
_____
_____
_____
_____
_____

Other Teaching Materials

_____
_____
_____
_____
_____
_____
_____
_____
_____
_____
_____

CHAPTER 14

Lesson 6

Writing the Conclusion

Pages 346–347

Lesson 6 Objectives
To recognize a strong conclusion and to use effective techniques for writing conclusions

THE LANGUAGE OF
LITERATURE Connect to *New Directions, On Being Seventeen, Bright, and Unable to Read,* Level 9.

Teach	Resources
Warm-Up	
___ Test Preparation	☐ 🏛 Daily Test Prep. p. DT41
Using the Pupil's Edition	
___ Purpose of Conclusions	☐ Pupil's Edition p. 346
___ Types of Conclusions	☐ Pupil's Edition p. 346

Practice and Apply

Using the Pupil's Edition	
___ Practice	☐ Pupil's Edition p. 347
Using Support Materials	
___ Types of Conclusions	☐ 🖥 Writing and Communication Masters p. 15
Using Support Materials	
___ Conclusion	☐ 🖥 SAE/ESL Side by Side p. 23

Assess and Close

Ongoing Assessment Options	
___ Assessment Information	☐ 🖥 Teacher's Guide to Assessment and Portfolio Use

Homework Assignments
_____
_____
_____
_____
_____
_____
_____
_____
_____
_____
_____

Other Teaching Materials
_____
_____
_____
_____
_____
_____
_____
_____
_____
_____
_____

CHAPTER 14

Preparing for Chapter 15

Resources

Warm-Up
___ Power Words
___ Write Away

☐ Pupil's Edition p. 350
☐ Pupil's Edition p. 351

Chapter Resources
___ Elaboration

☐ ⊗ Power Presentations
   CD-ROM Lesson 8

Lesson 1 # Why Elaborate?

Pages 352–353

Lesson 1 Objectives
To recognize and use elaboration in writing

 THE LANGUAGE OF LITERATURE Connect to *The Most Dangerous Game*, Level 9.

Teach

Resources

Warm-Up
___ Test Preparation

☐ ▦ Daily Test Prep. p. DT42

Using the Pupil's Edition
___ What's the Idea?
___ When Should You
     Elaborate?
___ How Can You Elaborate?

☐ Pupil's Edition p. 352
☐ Pupil's Edition p. 352

☐ Pupil's Edition p. 353

Using Support Materials
___ Adding Supporting Details

___ Elaboration Techniques

☐ Quick-Fix Grammar and Style
   Charts p. QF17
☐ Writing and Communication
   Skills p. WC8

Practice and Apply

Using the Pupil's Edition
___ Practice

☐ Pupil's Edition p. 353

Using Support Materials
___ Types of Elaboration

☐ ▤ Writing and Communication
   Masters p. 16

Customizing the Lesson
___ Verbs

☐ ○ SAE/ESL English Grammar
   Survival Kit pp. 24–26

Assess and Close

Ongoing Assessment Options
___ Assessment Information

☐ ▤ Teacher's Guide to Assessment and Portfolio Use

Homework Assignments
_____
_____
_____
_____
_____
_____
_____
_____
_____
_____

Other Teaching Materials
_____
_____
_____
_____
_____
_____
_____
_____
_____

CHAPTER 15

Copyright © McDougal Littell Inc.

Lesson 2

Supporting Details

Pages 354–355

Lesson 2 Objectives
To recognize and use sensory details, facts, and statistics in writing

THE LANGUAGE OF LITERATURE   Connect to *I Know Why the Caged Bird Sings*, Level 9.

Teach

Resources

Warm-Up
___ Test Preparation

☐ 🏛 Daily Test Prep. p. DT42

Using the Pupil's Edition
___ Elaborating with Sensory Details

☐ Pupil's Edition p. 354

___ Elaborating with Facts and Statistics

☐ Pupil's Edition p. 355

Using Support Materials
___ Observation Chart

☐ 🏛 Critical Thinking Graphic Organizers p. CT1

___ Adding Supporting Details

☐ 🏛 Quick-Fix Grammar and Style Charts p. QF17

___ Elaboration Techniques

☐ 🏛 Writing and Communication Skills p. WC8

Practice and Apply

Using the Pupil's Edition
___ Practice A

☐ Pupil's Edition p. 354

___ Practice B

☐ Pupil's Edition p. 355

Using Support Materials
___ Supporting Details

☐ 📖 Writing and Communication Masters p. 17

Assess and Close

Ongoing Assessment Options
___ Assessment Information

☐ 📖 Teacher's Guide to Assessment and Portfolio Use

Homework Assignments
_____
_____
_____
_____
_____
_____
_____
_____
_____

Other Teaching Materials
_____
_____
_____
_____
_____
_____
_____
_____
_____

CHAPTER 15

Lesson 3

Incidents, Examples and Quotations

Pages 356–357

Lesson 3 Objectives
To recognize and use incidents, examples and quotations in writing

Teach	Resources

Teach

Warm-Up
___ Test Preparation

☐ 🏛 Daily Test Prep. p. DT43

Using the Pupil's Edition
___ Elaborating With Incidents
___ Elaborating With Specific Examples
___ Elaborating With Quotations

☐ Pupil's Edition p. 356
☐ Pupil's Edition p. 356

☐ Pupil's Edition p. 357

Using Support Materials
___ Adding Supporting Details

___ Elaboration Techniques

☐ 🏛 Quick-Fix Grammar and Style Charts p. QF17
☐ 🏛 Writing and Communication Skills p. WC8

Practice and Apply

Using the Pupil's Edition
___ Practice A
___ Practice B
___ Practice C

☐ Pupil's Edition p. 356
☐ Pupil's Edition p. 357
☐ Pupil's Edition p. 357

Assess and Close

Ongoing Assessment Options
___ Assessment Information

☐ 📖 Teacher's Guide to Assessment and Portfolio Use

Homework Assignments

_____
_____
_____
_____
_____
_____
_____
_____
_____
_____

Other Teaching Materials

_____
_____
_____
_____
_____
_____
_____
_____
_____
_____

CHAPTER 15

Lesson 4

Elaborating With Visuals

Pages 358–359

Lesson 4 Objectives
To analyze visuals and to use them to enhance elaboration in writing

Teach	Resources
Warm-Up	
___ Test Preparation	☐ 📖 Daily Test Prep. p. DT43
Using the Pupil's Edition	
___ Illustrating a Definition	☐ Pupil's Edition p. 358
___ Illustrating a Process	☐ Pupil's Edition p. 358
___ Creating a Visual Display of Information	☐ Pupil's Edition p. 359
Using Support Materials	
___ Elaboration Techniques	☐ 📖 Writing and Communication Skills p. WC8

Practice and Apply

Using the Pupil's Edition	
___ Practice A	☐ Pupil's Edition p. 359
___ Practice B	☐ Pupil's Edition p. 359

Assess and Close

Ongoing Assessment Options	
___ Assessment Information	☐ 🎞 Teacher's Guide to Assessment and Portfolio Use

Homework Assignments

_____
_____
_____
_____
_____
_____
_____
_____
_____
_____

Other Teaching Materials

_____
_____
_____
_____
_____
_____
_____
_____
_____
_____

CHAPTER 15

Preparing for Chapter 16

Resources

Warm-Up
___ Power Words
___ Write Away

☐ Pupil's Edition p. 362
☐ Pupil's Edition p. 363

Chapter Resources
___ Revising Sentences

☐ 💿 Power Presentations
    CD-ROM Lesson 9

Lesson 1 — Empty and Padded Sentences

Pages 364–365

Lesson 1 Objectives
To recognize empty and padded sentences and to revise them

Teach

Resources

Warm-Up
___ Test Preparation

☐ 📘 Daily Test Prep. p. DT44

Using the Pupil's Edition
___ Filling Empty Sentences
___ Cutting the Fat from
    Padded Sentences

☐ Pupil's Edition p. 364
☐ Pupil's Edition p. 364

Using Support Materials
___ Improving Style

☐ 📘 Quick-Fix Grammar and
    Style Charts p. QF13–14

Practice and Apply

Using the Pupil's Edition
___ Practice

☐ Pupil's Edition p. 365

Using Support Materials
___ Filling Empty Sentences

☐ 🎞 Writing and Communication
    Masters p. 18

Assess and Close

Ongoing Assessment Options
___ Assessment Information

☐ 🎞 Teacher's Guide to Assess-
    ment and Portfolio Use

Homework Assignments

_____
_____
_____
_____
_____
_____
_____
_____
_____
_____

Other Teaching Materials

_____
_____
_____
_____
_____
_____
_____
_____
_____
_____
_____

CHAPTER 16

Copyright © McDougal Littell Inc.

Lesson 2

Stringy and Overloaded Sentences

Pages 366–367

Lesson 2 Objectives
To recognize sentences that contain loosely connected ideas joined by *and* and sentences that contain too much information, and to apply methods for revising them

Teach	Resources
Warm-Up	
___ Test Preparation	☐ 📖 Daily Test Prep. p. DT44
___ Untangling Stringy Sentences	☐ Pupil's Edition p. 366
___ Overloaded Sentences	☐ Pupil's Edition p. 366
Using Support Materials	
___ Improving Weak Sentences	☐ 📖 Quick-Fix Grammar and Style Charts p. QF13
Practice and Apply	
Using the Pupil's Edition	
___ Practice	☐ Pupil's Edition p. 367
Using Support Materials	
___ Stringy and Overloaded Sentences	☐ 📖 Writing and Communication Masters p. 19
Assess and Close	
Ongoing Assessment Options	
___ Assessment Information	☐ 📖 Teacher's Guide to Assessment and Portfolio Use

Homework Assignments	Other Teaching Materials
_____	_____
_____	_____
_____	_____
_____	_____
_____	_____
_____	_____
_____	_____
_____	_____
_____	_____
_____	_____

CHAPTER 16

Lesson 3

Combining Sentences

Pages 368–371

Lesson 3 Objectives
To identify sentences that can be combined and to apply techniques for combining sentences

Teach	Resources
Warm-Up ___ Test Preparation	☐ 🏛 Daily Test Prep. p. DT45
Using the Pupil's Edition ___ Why Combine Sentences? ___ Combining Whole Sentences ___ Combining Sentence Parts ___ Combining with *That, Which, Who*	☐ Pupil's Edition p. 368 ☐ Pupil's Edition p. 368 ☐ Pupil's Edition p. 369 ☐ Pupil's Edition p. 370
Using Support Materials ___ Revising Sentences	☐ 🏛 Visual Grammar™ Tiles, Lessons 23–25

Practice and Apply

Using the Pupil's Edition ___ Practice	☐ Pupil's Edition p. 371
Using Support Materials ___ Combining Sentences and Sentence Parts	☐ 📖 Writing and Communication Masters p. 20
Customizing the Lesson ___ Combining Short Sentences	☐ 🎧 SAE/ESL Side by Side p. 27

Assess and Close

Ongoing Assessment Options ___ Assessment Information	☐ 📖 Teacher's Guide to Assessment and Portfolio Use

Homework Assignments
_____
_____
_____
_____
_____
_____
_____
_____
_____

Other Teaching Materials
_____
_____
_____
_____
_____
_____
_____
_____

CHAPTER 16

Lesson 4

Inserting Words and Phrases

Pages 372–373

Lesson 4 Objectives
To identify sentences that can be combined and to combine sentences by inserting single words or phrases or by changing sentences into appositives

Teach	Resources
Warm-Up ___ Test Preparation	☐ 🏛 Daily Test Prep. p. DT45
Using the Pupil's Edition ___ Combining with Words and Phrases ___ Combining with Appositives	☐ Pupil's Edition p. 372 ☐ Pupil's Edition p. 373
Using Support Materials ___ Combining by Inserting Words and Phrases	☐ 🏛 Visual Grammar™ Tiles, Lesson 26

Practice and Apply

Using the Pupil's Edition ___ Practice	☐ Pupil's Edition p. 373
Using Support Materials ___ Revising Sentences	☐ 📖 Writing and Communication Masters pp. 21–22
Customizing the Lesson ___ Combining Sentences Using Words, Phrases, Appositives	☐ ◯ SAE/ESL Side by Side p. 28

Assess and Close

Ongoing Assessment Options ___ Assessment Information	☐ 📖 Teacher's Guide to Assessment and Portfolio Use

Homework Assignments

_____
_____
_____
_____
_____
_____
_____
_____

Other Teaching Materials

_____
_____
_____
_____
_____
_____
_____
_____
_____

CHAPTER 16

Lesson 5

Using Active and Passive Voice

Pages 374–375

Lesson 5 Objectives
To recognize and use the active voice and the passive voice in writing

Teach	Resources
Warm-Up	
___ Test Preparation	☐ 📖 Daily Test Prep. p. DT46
Using the Pupil's Edition	
___ Using Active Voice	☐ Pupil's Edition p. 374
___ Using Passive Voice	☐ Pupil's Edition p. 375
Using Support Materials	
___ Using Active and Passive Voice	☐ 📖 Quick-Fix Grammar and Style Charts p. QF12
___ Passive Voice	☐ 📖 Visual Grammar™ Tiles, Lesson 16

Practice and Apply

Using the Pupil's Edition	
___ Practice	☐ Pupil's Edition p. 375
Using Support Materials	
___ Using Active and Passive Voice	☐ 📖 Writing and Communication Masters pp. 23

Assess and Close

Ongoing Assessment Options	
___ Assessment Information	☐ 📖 Teacher's Guide to Assessment and Portfolio Use

Homework Assignments
_____
_____
_____
_____
_____
_____
_____
_____
_____
_____

Other Teaching Materials
_____
_____
_____
_____
_____
_____
_____
_____
_____
_____

CHAPTER 16

CHAPTER 17

Preparing for Chapter 17 | Resources

Warm-Up
___ Power Words
___ Write Away

☐ Pupil's Edition p. 378
☐ Pupil's Edition p. 379

Chapter Resources
___ Developing Style

☐ 💿 Power Presentations
CD-ROM Lesson 10

Lesson 1

What Is Style?

Pages 380–381

Lesson 1 Objectives
To recognize elements of style and to apply them to literary models

THE LANGUAGE OF LITERATURE Connect to *The Possibility of Evil, My Wonder Horse,* Level 9.

Teach | Resources

Warm-Up
___ Test Preparation

☐ 🏛 Daily Test Prep. p. DT46

Using the Pupil's Edition
___ Recognizing Style
___ Describing Style

☐ Pupil's Edition p. 380
☐ Pupil's Edition p. 380

Using Support Materials
___ Varying Sentence Structure

☐ 🏛 Visual Grammar™ Tiles,
Lesson 27

Practice and Apply

Using the Pupil's Edition
___ Practice

☐ Pupil's Edition p. 381

Using Support Materials
___ Recognizing Writing Styles

☐ 📰 Writing and Communication
Masters p. 24

Assess and Close

Ongoing Assessment Options
___ Assessment Information

☐ 📰 Teacher's Guide to Assessment and Portfolio Use

Homework Assignments
_____
_____
_____
_____
_____
_____
_____
_____
_____

Other Teaching Materials
_____
_____
_____
_____
_____
_____
_____
_____

Lesson 2

Word Choice

Pages 382–383

Lesson 2 Objectives

To understand precise word choice and connotative and denotative meaning, and to apply good word choice in writing

 THE LANGUAGE OF LITERATURE Connect to *Full Circle,* Level 9.

Teach	Resources
Warm-Up	
___ Test Preparation	☐ 🏛 Daily Test Prep. p. DT47
Using the Pupil's Edition	
___ Choosing Precise Words	☐ Pupil's Edition p. 382
___ Denotative and Connotative Meanings	☐ Pupil's Edition p. 383
Using Support Materials	
___ Using Precise Words	☐ 🏛 Quick-Fix Grammar and Style Charts p. QF19

Practice and Apply

Using the Pupil's Edition	
___ Practice A	☐ Pupil's Edition p. 382
___ Practice B	☐ Pupil's Edition p. 383
Using Support Materials	
___ Choosing Precise Words	☐ 📄 Writing and Communication Masters p. 25

Assess and Close

Ongoing Assessment Options	
___ Assessment Information	☐ 📄 Teacher's Guide to Assessment and Portfolio Use

---

Homework Assignments

_____
_____
_____
_____
_____
_____
_____
_____

Other Teaching Materials

_____
_____
_____
_____
_____
_____
_____
_____

Lesson 3 — Varieties of Language

Pages 384–385

Lesson 3 Objectives
To recognize differences between formal and informal language and to apply this information in writing

Teach	Resources
Warm-Up	
___ Test Preparation	☐ 🏛 Daily Test Prep. p. DT47
Using the Pupil's Edition	
___ Matching Language to Audience and Purpose	☐ Pupil's Edition p. 384
___ Formal and Informal Language	☐ Pupil's Edition p. 384
___ Varieties of Informal Language	☐ Pupil's Edition p. 385
Using Support Materials	
___ Avoiding Clichés and Slang	☐ 🏛 Quick-Fix Grammar and Style Charts p. QF18

Practice and Apply

Using the Pupil's Edition	
___ Practice	☐ Pupil's Edition p. 385
Using Support Materials	
___ Varieties of Language	☐ 📖 Writing and Communication Masters p. 26

Assess and Close

Ongoing Assessment Options	
___ Assessment Information	☐ 📖 Teacher's Guide to Assessment and Portfolio Use

Homework Assignments
_____
_____
_____
_____
_____
_____
_____
_____

Other Teaching Materials
_____
_____
_____
_____
_____
_____
_____
_____

CHAPTER 17

Lesson 4

Imagery and Figures of Speech

Pages 386–389

Lesson 4 Objectives
To recognize imagery and figures of speech and to use them in writing

THE LANGUAGE OF **LITERATURE** Connect to *Two Kinds, The Scarlet Ibis, Black Boy, The Cultural Worker*, Level 9.

Teach

Warm-Up
___ Test Preparation

Using the Pupil's Edition
___ Imagery
___ Figures of Speech

Using Support Materials
___ Sensory Word List

Practice and Apply

Using the Pupil's Edition
___ Practice A
___ Practice B
___ Practice C
___ Practice D

Using Support Materials
___ Imagery and Figures of Speech

Assess and Close

Ongoing Assessment Options
___ Assessment Information

Resources

☐ Daily Test Prep. p. DT48

☐ Pupil's Edition p. 386
☐ Pupil's Edition p. 387

☐ Writing and Communication Skills p. WC9

☐ Pupil's Edition p. 386
☐ Pupil's Edition p. 388
☐ Pupil's Edition p. 389
☐ Pupil's Edition p. 389

☐ Writing and Communication Masters p. 27

☐ Teacher's Guide to Assessment and Portfolio Use

Homework Assignments
_____
_____
_____
_____
_____
_____
_____
_____
_____

Other Teaching Materials
_____
_____
_____
_____
_____
_____
_____
_____

Lesson 5

Tone and Voice

Pages 390–391

Lesson 5 Objectives
To understand tone and voice and to use them in writing

 **THE LANGUAGE OF LITERATURE** Connect to *A Christmas Memory,* Level 9.

Teach	Resources
Warm-Up ___ Test Preparation	☐ 🏛 Daily Test Prep. p. DT48
Using the Pupil's Edition ___ Creating Tone ___ Recognizing Your Own Voice	☐ Pupil's Edition p. 390 ☐ Pupil's Edition p. 391
Practice and Apply	
Using the Pupil's Edition ___ Practice A ___ Practice B	☐ Pupil's Edition p. 390 ☐ Pupil's Edition p. 391
Assess and Close	
Ongoing Assessment Options ___ Assessment Information	☐ 📋 Teacher's Guide to Assessment and Portfolio Use

Homework Assignments

_____
_____
_____
_____
_____
_____
_____
_____
_____
_____

Other Teaching Materials

_____
_____
_____
_____
_____
_____
_____
_____
_____
_____

Lesson 1 — Personal Narrative

Pages 396–403

Lesson 1 Objectives
To analyze and write an effective personal narrative

THE LANGUAGE OF **LITERATURE** Connect to Personal Narrative Writing Workshop, Level 9.

Teach	Resources
Warm-Up	
___ Test Preparation	☐ Daily Test Prep. p. DT49
Using the Pupil's Edition	
___ Learn What It Is	☐ Pupil's Edition p. 396
___ See How It's Done	☐ Pupil's Edition p. 397
Using Support Materials	
___ Personal Narrative at a Glance	☐ Basics in a Box p. BB1
___ Cluster Diagram, Spider Map, Sequence Chain	☐ Critical Thinking Graphic Organizers pp. CT3, 5, 9
___ Run-On Sentences	☐ Quick-Fix Grammar and Style Charts p. QF2
___ Personal Narrative Model	☐ Revising, Editing, and Proofreading Models pp. RE1–4

Practice and Apply

Using the Pupil's Edition	
Do It Yourself	
___ Prewriting	☐ Pupil's Edition p. 399
___ Drafting	☐ Pupil's Edition p. 399
___ Revising	☐ Pupil's Edition p. 400
___ Editing and Proofreading	☐ Pupil's Edition p. 400
___ Sharing and Reflecting	☐ Pupil's Edition p. 400
Using Support Materials	
___ Prewriting	☐ Writing and Communication Masters p. 28
___ Drafting and Elaboration	☐ Writing and Communication Masters p. 29
___ Peer Response Guide	☐ Writing and Communication Masters pp. 30–31
___ Revising, Editing, and Proofreading	☐ Writing and Communication Masters p. 32
___ Student Models (Strong, Average, Weak)	☐ Writing and Communication Masters pp. 33–38 (also printed in Assessment Masters pp. 146–151)

Homework Assignments
_____
_____
_____
_____
_____
_____
_____
_____
_____

Other Teaching Materials
_____
_____
_____
_____
_____
_____
_____
_____
_____
_____

Lesson 1

Personal Narrative *(continued)*

Pages 396–403

Resources

Using Technology
___ Personal Narrative
___ Additional Writing Prompts

Customizing the Lesson
___ Personal Narrative

☐ ⊙ Writing Coach CD-ROM
☐ ⬤ mcdougallittell.com

☐ ▦ SAE/ESL Side by Side
pp. 31–42

Assess and Close

Using Technology
___ Rubric for Evaluation

___ Writing Prompts
___ Rubrics

Ongoing Assessment Options
___ Assessment Information

☐ ▦ Writing and Communication
Masters p. 39
☐ ▦ Assessment Masters p. 130
☐ ▦ Assessment Masters p. 138

☐ ▦ Teacher's Guide to Assessment and Portfolio Use

Publish

Using Technology
___ Writing Center

☐ ⬤ mcdougallittell.com

Homework Assignments
_____
_____
_____
_____
_____
_____
_____
_____
_____
_____
_____
_____

Other Teaching Materials
_____
_____
_____
_____
_____
_____
_____
_____
_____
_____
_____
_____

Lesson 1

Character Sketch

Pages 404–411

Lesson 1 Objectives
To analyze and write an effective character sketch

 THE LANGUAGE OF **LITERATURE** Connect to Character Sketch Writing Workshop, Level 9.

Teach

Warm-Up
___ Test Preparation

Using the Pupil's Edition
___ Learn What It Is
___ See How It's Done

Using Support Materials
___ Character Sketch at a Glance
___ Vertical Category Chart

___ Varying Sentence Beginnings, Varying Sentence Structure
___ Character Sketch Model

Practice and Apply

Using the Pupil's Edition
Do It Yourself
___ Prewriting
___ Drafting
___ Revising
___ Editing and Proofreading
___ Sharing and Reflecting

Using Support Materials
___ Prewriting

___ Drafting and Elaboration

___ Peer Response Guide

___ Revising, Editing, and Proofreading
___ Student Models (Strong, Average, Weak)

Resources

☐ 📖 Daily Test Prep. p. DT49

☐ Pupil's Edition p. 404
☐ Pupil's Edition p. 405

☐ 📖 Basics in a Box p. BB2

☐ 📖 Critical Thinking Graphic Organizers p. CT11
☐ 📖 Quick-Fix Grammar and Style Charts pp. QF15–16

☐ 📖 Revising, Editing, and Proofreading Models pp. RE5–8

☐ Pupil's Edition p. 407
☐ Pupil's Edition p. 407
☐ Pupil's Edition p. 408
☐ Pupil's Edition p. 408
☐ Pupil's Edition p. 408

☐ 📖 Writing and Communication Masters p. 40
☐ 📖 Writing and Communication Masters p.41
☐ 📖 Writing and Communication Masters pp. 42–43
☐ 📖 Writing and Communication Masters p. 44
☐ 📖 Writing and Communication Masters pp. 45–50 (also printed in Assessment Masters pp. 152–157)

Homework Assignments
_____
_____
_____
_____
_____
_____
_____
_____
_____

Other Teaching Materials
_____
_____
_____
_____
_____
_____
_____
_____
_____

Teacher _____ Class _____ Date _____

Lesson 1 **Character Sketch** *(continued)*   *Pages 404–411*

Resources

Using Technology
___ Run-On Sentences

___ Additional Writing Prompts

Customizing the Lesson
___ Character Sketch

☐ ⊗ Grammar Coach CD-ROM, Lesson 2
☐ ✐ mcdougallittell.com

☐ ▦ SAE/ESL Side by Side pp. 43–54

Assess and Close

Using Technology
___ Rubric for Evaluation

___ Writing Prompts
___ Rubrics

Ongoing Assessment Options
___ Assessment Information

☐ ▦ Writing and Communication Masters p. 51
☐ ▦ Assessment Masters p. 131
☐ ▦ Assessment Masters p. 139

☐ ▦ Teacher's Guide to Assessment and Portfolio Use

Publish

Using Technology
___ Writing Center

☐ ✐ mcdougallittell.com

CHAPTER 19

Homework Assignments

_____
_____
_____
_____
_____
_____
_____
_____
_____
_____
_____
_____

Other Teaching Materials

_____
_____
_____
_____
_____
_____
_____
_____
_____
_____
_____
_____

Lesson 1 # Response to Literature

Pages 412–419

Lesson 1 Objectives
To analyze and write an effective personal response to literature

THE LANGUAGE OF LITERATURE Connect to Response to Literature Writing Workshop, Level 9.

Teach	Resources
Warm-Up	
___ Test Preparation	☐ 🏛 Daily Test Prep. p. DT50
Using the Pupil's Edition	
___ Learn What It Is	☐ Pupil's Edition p. 412
___ See How It's Done	☐ Pupil's Edition p. 413
Using Support Materials	
___ Response to Literature at a Glance	☐ 🏛 Basics in a Box p. BB3
___ Main Idea Analysis Frame	☐ 🏛 Critical Thinking Graphic Organizers p. CT13
___ Subject-Verb Agreement 1–2	☐ 🏛 Quick-Fix Grammar and Style Charts pp. QF3–4
___ Response to Literature Model	☐ 🏛 Revising, Editing, and Proofreading Models pp. RE9–12
___ Organizing an Expository Composition, Thesis Statement	☐ 🏛 Writing and Communication Skills pp. WC5, 7

Practice and Apply

Using the Pupil's Edition	
Do It Yourself	
___ Prewriting	☐ Pupil's Edition p. 415
___ Drafting	☐ Pupil's Edition p. 415
___ Revising	☐ Pupil's Edition p. 416
___ Editing and Proofreading	☐ Pupil's Edition p. 416
___ Sharing and Reflecting	☐ Pupil's Edition p. 416
Using Support Materials	
___ Prewriting	☐ 📼 Writing and Communication Masters p. 52
___ Drafting and Elaboration	☐ 📼 Writing and Communication Masters p. 53
___ Peer Response Guide	☐ 📼 Writing and Communication Masters pp. 54–55
___ Revising, Editing, and Proofreading	☐ 📼 Writing and Communication Masters p. 56
___ Student Models (Strong, Average, Weak)	☐ 📼 Writing and Communication Masters pp. 57–62 (also printed in Assessment Masters pp. 158–163)

Homework Assignments
_____
_____
_____
_____
_____
_____
_____
_____
_____

Other Teaching Materials
_____
_____
_____
_____
_____
_____
_____
_____

CHAPTER 20

Lesson 1

Response to Literature *(continued)*

Resources

Using Technology
___ Subject and Verb Agreement II
___ Additional Writing Prompts

☐ 💿 Grammar Coach CD-ROM, Lesson 5
☐ 🖱 mcdougallittell.com

Customizing the Lesson
___ Response to Literature

☐ 📖 SAE/ESL Side by Side pp. 55–66

Assess and Close

Using Technology
___ Rubric for Evaluation

☐ 📖 Writing and Communication Masters p. 63

___ Writing Prompts
___ Rubrics

☐ 📖 Assessment Masters p. 132
☐ 📖 Assessment Masters p. 140

Ongoing Assessment Options
___ Assessment Information

☐ 📖 Teacher's Guide to Assessment and Portfolio Use

Publish

Using Technology
___ Writing Center

☐ 🖱 mcdougallittell.com

CHAPTER 20

Homework Assignments

_____
_____
_____
_____
_____
_____
_____
_____
_____

Other Teaching Materials

_____
_____
_____
_____
_____
_____
_____
_____
_____

Lesson 1

Process Explanation

Pages 420–427

Lesson 1 Objectives
To analyze and write a process explanation

 THE LANGUAGE OF LITERATURE Connect to Process Description Writing Workshop, Level 9.

Teach

Warm-Up
___ Test Preparation

Using the Pupil's Edition
___ Learn What It Is
___ See How It's Done

Using Support Materials
___ Process Explanation at a Glance
___ Sequence Chain

___ Process Explanation Model

Resources

☐ 🏛 Daily Test Prep. p. DT50

☐ Pupil's Edition p. 420
☐ Pupil's Edition p. 421

☐ 🏛 Basics in a Box p. BB4

☐ 🏛 Critical Thinking Graphic Organizers p. CT9
☐ 🏛 Revising, Editing, and Proofreading Models pp. RE13–16

Practice and Apply

Using the Pupil's Edition
Do It Yourself
___ Prewriting
___ Drafting
___ Revising
___ Editing and Proofreading
___ Sharing and Reflecting

Using Support Materials
___ Prewriting

___ Drafting and Elaboration

___ Peer Response Guide

___ Revising, Editing, and Proofreading
___ Student Models (Strong, Average, Weak)

☐ Pupil's Edition p. 423
☐ Pupil's Edition p. 423
☐ Pupil's Edition p. 424
☐ Pupil's Edition p. 424
☐ Pupil's Edition p. 424

☐ 📖 Writing and Communication Masters p. 64
☐ 📖 Writing and Communication Masters p. 64
☐ 📖 Writing and Communication Masters pp. 66–67
☐ 📖 Writing and Communication Masters p. 68
☐ 📖 Writing and Communication Masters pp. 69–74 (also printed in Assessment Masters pp. 164–169)

Homework Assignments
_____
_____
_____
_____
_____
_____
_____
_____

Other Teaching Materials
_____
_____
_____
_____
_____
_____
_____
_____

CHAPTER 21

Lesson 1

Process Explanation *(continued)*

Pages 420–427

Resources

Using Technology
___ Description of a Process
___ Additional Writing Prompts

☐ ⊛ Writing Coach CD-ROM
☐ ✐ mcdougallittell.com

Customizing the Lesson
___ Process Explanation

☐ ▦ SAE/ESL Side by Side pp. 67–78

Assess and Close

Using Technology
___ Rubric for Evaluation

___ Writing Prompts
___ Rubrics

☐ ▦ Writing and Communication Masters p. 75
☐ ▦ Assessment Masters p. 133
☐ ▦ Assessment Masters p. 141

Ongoing Assessment Options
___ Assessment Information

☐ ▦ Teacher's Guide to Assessment and Portfolio Use

Publish

Using Technology
___ Writing Center

☐ ✐ mcdougallittell.com

CHAPTER 21

Homework Assignments

_____
_____
_____
_____
_____
_____
_____
_____
_____
_____

Other Teaching Materials

_____
_____
_____
_____
_____
_____
_____
_____
_____
_____

Lesson 1

Comparison-Contrast Essay

Pages 428–435

Lesson 1 Objectives
To analyze and write a compare-and-contrast essay

THE LANGUAGE OF LITERATURE Connect to Comparison-Contrast Writing Workshop, Level 9.

Teach

Warm-Up
___ Test Preparation

Using the Pupil's Edition
___ Learn What It Is
___ See How It's Done

Using Support Materials
___ Comparison-Contrast Essay at a Glance
___ Compare/Contrast Chart

___ Sentence Fragments

___ Comparison-Contrast Essay Model

___ Transitional Words, Organizing an Expository Composition

Practice and Apply

Using the Pupil's Edition
Do It Yourself
___ Prewriting
___ Drafting
___ Revising
___ Editing and Proofreading
___ Sharing and Reflecting

Using Support Materials
___ Prewriting

___ Drafting and Elaboration

___ Peer Response Guide

___ Revising, Editing, and Proofreading
___ Student Models (Strong, Average, Weak)

Resources

☐ Daily Test Prep. p. DT51

☐ Pupil's Edition p. 428
☐ Pupil's Edition p. 429

☐ Basics in a Box p. BB5

☐ Critical Thinking Graphic Organizers p. CT17
☐ Quick-Fix Grammar and Style Charts pp. QF1
☐ Revising, Editing, and Proofreading Models pp. RE17–20
☐ Writing and Communication Skills pp. WC4–5

☐ Pupil's Edition p. 431
☐ Pupil's Edition p. 431
☐ Pupil's Edition p. 432
☐ Pupil's Edition p. 432
☐ Pupil's Edition p. 432

☐ Writing and Communication Masters p. 76
☐ Writing and Communication Masters p. 77
☐ Writing and Communication Masters pp. 78–79
☐ Writing and Communication Masters p. 80
☐ Writing and Communication Masters pp. 81–86 (also printed in Assessment Masters pp. 170–175)

Homework Assignments
_____
_____
_____
_____
_____
_____
_____
_____
_____

Other Teaching Materials
_____
_____
_____
_____
_____
_____
_____
_____

CHAPTER 22

Lesson 1

Comparison-Contrast Essay *(continued)*

Pages 428–435

Resources

Using Technology
___ Sentence Fragments

___ Comparison-Contrast
___ Additional Writing Prompts

Customizing the Lesson
___ Compare-and-Contrast
Essay

☐ ⊛ Grammar Coach CD-ROM,
Lesson 1
☐ ⊛ Writing Coach CD-ROM
☐ ⬙ mcdougallittell.com

☐ ▤ SAE/ESL Side by Side
pp. 79–90

Assess and Close

Using Technology
___ Rubric for Evaluation

___ Writing Prompts
___ Rubrics

Ongoing Assessment Options
___ Assessment Information

☐ ▤ Writing and Communication
Masters p. 87
☐ ▤ Assessment Masters p. 134
☐ ▤ Assessment Masters p. 142

☐ ▤ Teacher's Guide to Assessment and Portfolio Use

Publish

Using Technology
___ Writing Center

☐ ⬙ mcdougallittell.com

Homework Assignments

_____
_____
_____
_____
_____
_____
_____
_____
_____
_____

Other Teaching Materials

_____
_____
_____
_____
_____
_____
_____
_____
_____
_____

CHAPTER 22

Lesson 1

Opinion Statement

Pages 436–445

Lesson 1 Objectives
To analyze and write an opinion statement

 THE LANGUAGE OF **LITERATURE** Connect to Opinion Statement Writing Workshop, Level 9.

Teach	Resources
Warm-Up	
___ Test Preparation	☐ 🏛 Daily Test Prep. p. DT51
Using the Pupil's Edition	
___ Learn What It Is	☐ Pupil's Edition p. 436
___ See How It's Done	☐ Pupil's Edition p. 437
Using Support Materials	
___ Opinion Statement at a Glance	☐ 🏛 Basics in a Box p. BB6
___ Main Idea Analysis Frame	☐ 🏛 Critical Thinking Graphic Organizers p. CT13
___ Sentence Fragments	☐ 🏛 Quick-Fix Grammar and Style Charts pp. QF1
___ Opinion Statement Model	☐ 🏛 Revising, Editing, and Proofreading Models pp. RE21–24
___ Organizing an Expository Composition	☐ 🏛 Writing and Communication Skills pp. WC5

Practice and Apply

Using the Pupil's Edition
Do It Yourself

___ Prewriting	☐ Pupil's Edition p. 439
___ Drafting	☐ Pupil's Edition p. 440
___ Revising	☐ Pupil's Edition p. 441
___ Editing and Proofreading	☐ Pupil's Edition p. 442
___ Sharing and Reflecting	☐ Pupil's Edition p. 442

Using Support Materials

___ Prewriting	☐ 📖 Writing and Communication Masters p. 88
___ Drafting and Elaboration	☐ 📖 Writing and Communication Masters p. 89
___ Peer Response Guide	☐ 📖 Writing and Communication Masters pp. 90–91
___ Revising, Editing, and Proofreading	☐ 📖 Writing and Communication Masters p. 92
___ Student Models (Strong, Average, Weak)	☐ 📖 Writing and Communication Masters pp. 93–98 (also printed in Assessment Masters pp. 176–181)

Homework Assignments
_____
_____
_____
_____
_____
_____
_____
_____
_____

Other Teaching Materials
_____
_____
_____
_____
_____
_____
_____
_____

CHAPTER 23

Lesson 1

Opinion Statement *(continued)*

Pages 436–445

Resources

Using Technology
___ Sentence Fragments

___ Additional Writing Prompts

☐ 💿 Grammar Coach CD-ROM, Lesson 1

☐ 🌐 mcdougallittell.com

Customizing the Lesson
___ Opinion Statement

☐ 📷 SAE/ESL Side by Side pp. 91–102

Assess and Close

Using Technology
___ Rubric for Evaluation

___ Writing Prompts
___ Rubrics

☐ 📷 Writing and Communication Masters p. 99

☐ 📷 Assessment Masters p. 135
☐ 📷 Assessment Masters p. 143

Ongoing Assessment Options
___ Assessment Information

☐ 📷 Teacher's Guide to Assessment and Portfolio Use

Publish

Using Technology
___ Writing Center

☐ 🌐 mcdougallittell.com

Homework Assignments

_____
_____
_____
_____
_____
_____
_____
_____
_____
_____

Other Teaching Materials

_____
_____
_____
_____
_____
_____
_____
_____
_____
_____

CHAPTER 23

Lesson 1

Short Story

Pages 446–455

Lesson 1 Objectives

To understand the structure of and to write a short story
To learn about the elements of a poem and a dramatic scene

THE LANGUAGE OF
LITERATURE Connect to Short Story Writing Workshop, Level 9.

Teach

Warm-Up
___ Test Preparation

Using the Pupil's Edition
___ Learn What It Is
___ See How It's Done

Using Support Materials
___ Short Story at a Glance
___ Cluster Diagram, Vertical
Category Chart
___ Short Story Model

Resources

☐ 🏛 Daily Test Prep. p. DT52

☐ Pupil's Edition p. 446
☐ Pupil's Edition p. 447

☐ 🏛 Basics in a Box p. BB7
☐ 🏛 Critical Thinking Graphic
Organizers pp. CT3, 9
☐ 🏛 Revising, Editing, and
Proofreading Models
pp. RE25–28

Practice and Apply

Using the Pupil's Edition
Do It Yourself
___ Prewriting
___ Drafting
___ Revising
___ Editing and Proofreading
___ Sharing and Reflecting

Using Support Materials
___ Prewriting

___ Drafting and Elaboration

___ Peer Response Guide

___ Revising, Editing, and
Proofreading
___ Student Models (Strong,
Average, Weak)

☐ Pupil's Edition p. 449
☐ Pupil's Edition p. 449
☐ Pupil's Edition p. 450
☐ Pupil's Edition p. 450
☐ Pupil's Edition p. 450

☐ 📓 Writing and Communication
Masters p. 100
☐ 📓 Writing and Communication
Masters p. 101
☐ 📓 Writing and Communication
Masters pp. 102–103
☐ 📓 Writing and Communication
Masters p. 104
☐ 📓 Writing and Communication
Masters pp. 105–110
(also printed in Assessment
Masters pp. 182–187)

Homework Assignments
_____
_____
_____
_____
_____
_____
_____
_____
_____

Other Teaching Materials
_____
_____
_____
_____
_____
_____
_____
_____
_____

CHAPTER 24

Lesson 1

Short Story *(continued)*

Pages 446–455

Resources

Using Technology
___ Short Story
___ Additional Writing Prompts

Customizing the Lesson
___ Short Story

☐ ⊚ Writing Coach CD-ROM
☐ ◉ mcdougallittell.com

☐ ▦ SAE/ESL Side by Side
    pp. 103–114

Assess and Close

Using Technology
___ Rubric for Evaluation

___ Writing Prompts
___ Rubrics

Ongoing Assessment Options
___ Assessment Information

☐ ▦ Writing and Communication
    Masters p. 111
☐ ▦ Assessment Masters p. 136
☐ ▦ Assessment Masters p. 144

☐ ▦ Teacher's Guide to Assess-
    ment and Portfolio Use

Publish

Using Technology
___ Writing Center

☐ ◉ mcdougallittell.com

Homework Assignments

_____
_____
_____
_____
_____
_____
_____
_____
_____
_____

Other Teaching Materials

_____
_____
_____
_____
_____
_____
_____
_____
_____
_____

CHAPTER 24

Research Report

Lesson 1

Pages 456–471

Lesson 1 Objectives

To analyze a model research report and to produce an original research report

 THE LANGUAGE OF LITERATURE   Connect to Research Report Writing Workshop, Level 9.

Teach	Resources

Warm-Up
___ Test Preparation
    ☐ 📕 Daily Test Prep. p. DT52

Using the Pupil's Edition
___ Learn What It Is
    ☐ Pupil's Edition p. 456
___ See How It's Done
    ☐ Pupil's Edition p. 457

Using Support Materials
___ Research Report at a Glance
    ☐ 📕 Basics in a Box p. BB8
___ Using Precise Words
    ☐ 📕 Quick-Fix Grammar and Style Charts pp. QF19
___ Research Report Model
    ☐ 📕 Revising, Editing, and Proofreading Models pp. RE29–36
___ Writing Skills
    ☐ 📕 Writing and Communication Skills pp. WC5, 7

Practice and Apply

Using the Pupil's Edition
Do It Yourself
___ Developing a Research Plan
    ☐ Pupil's Edition p. 459
___ Using and Documenting Sources
    ☐ Pupil's Edition p. 461
___ Crafting a Good Thesis Statement
    ☐ Pupil's Edition p. 464
___ Organizing and Outlining
    ☐ Pupil's Edition p. 464
___ Drafting
    ☐ Pupil's Edition p. 465
___ Revising
    ☐ Pupil's Edition p. 469
___ Editing
    ☐ Pupil's Edition p. 469
___ Proofreading
    ☐ Pupil's Edition p. 469

Using Support Materials
___ Prewriting
    ☐ 📗 Writing and Communication Masters p. 112
___ Drafting and Elaboration
    ☐ 📗 Writing and Communication Masters p. 113
___ Peer Response Guide
    ☐ 📗 Writing and Communication Masters pp. 114–115
___ Revising, Editing, and Proofreading
    ☐ 📗 Writing and Communication Masters p. 116

Homework Assignments
_____
_____
_____
_____
_____
_____
_____
_____

Other Teaching Materials
_____
_____
_____
_____
_____
_____
_____
_____

Research Report *(continued)*

Pages 456–471

___ Student Models (Strong, Average, Weak)

Using Technology
___ Research Paper
___ Additional Writing Prompts

Customizing the Lesson
___ Research Paper

Assess and Close

Using Technology
___ Rubric for Evaluation

___ Writing Prompts
___ Rubrics

Ongoing Assessment Options
___ Assessment Information

Publish

Using Technology
___ Writing Center

Resources

☐ 🖵 Writing and Communication Masters pp. 117–122 (also printed in Assessment Masters pp. 188–193)

☐ 💿 Writing Coach CD-ROM
☐ 🌐 mcdougallittell.com

☐ 🖵 SAE/ESL Side by Side pp. 115–129

☐ 🖵 Writing and Communication Masters p. 123
☐ 🖵 Assessment Masters p. 137
☐ 🖵 Assessment Masters p. 145

☐ 🖵 Teacher's Guide to Assessment and Portfolio Use

☐ 🌐 mcdougallittell.com

Homework Assignments

_____
_____
_____
_____
_____
_____
_____
_____
_____
_____
_____

Other Teaching Materials

_____
_____
_____
_____
_____
_____
_____
_____
_____
_____
_____

Preparing for Chapter 26 | Resources

Warm-Up
___ Power Words
___ Write Away

☐ Pupil's Edition p. 474
☐ Pupil's Edition p. 475

Lesson 1

The Library and Media Center

Pages 476–477

Lesson 1 Objectives
To identify and use available resources for conducting research

Teach | Resources

Warm-Up
___ Test Preparation

☐ 📖 Daily Test Prep. p. DT53

Using the Pupil's Edition
___ Using Catalogs
___ Special Services
___ The Library Collection

☐ Pupil's Edition p. 476
☐ Pupil's Edition p. 476
☐ Pupil's Edition p. 477

Practice and Apply

Using Support Materials
___ Organization of the Library

☐ 📖 Writing and Communication Masters p. 124

Assess and Close

Ongoing Assessment Options
___ Assessment Information

☐ 📖 Teacher's Guide to Assessment and Portfolio Use

Homework Assignments

_____
_____
_____
_____
_____
_____
_____
_____
_____
_____

Other Teaching Materials

_____
_____
_____
_____
_____
_____
_____
_____
_____
_____

Lesson 2

Using Reference Works

Pages 478–479

Lesson 2 Objectives
To identify and use print and electronic reference resources

Teach

Resources

Warm-Up
___ Test Preparation

☐ 🏛 Daily Test Prep. p. DT53

Using the Pupil's Edition
___ Using Print References
___ Using Databases
___ Using Electronic
     References

☐ Pupil's Edition p. 478
☐ Pupil's Edition p. 478
☐ Pupil's Edition p. 479

Practice and Apply

Using Support Materials
___ Using Reference Works

☐ 🖽 Writing and Communication
     Masters p. 125

Assess and Close

Ongoing Assessment Options
___ Assessment Information

☐ 🖽 Teacher's Guide to Assess-
     ment and Portfolio Use

Homework Assignments

_____
_____
_____
_____
_____
_____
_____
_____
_____

Other Teaching Materials

_____
_____
_____
_____
_____
_____
_____
_____
_____

Lesson 3

Searching the Web

Pages 480–481

Lesson 3 Objectives
To learn how to use the World Wide Web and to consult Web resources when researching topics

Teach	Resources
Warm-Up ___ Test Preparation	☐ 🏛 Daily Test Prep. p. DT54
Using the Pupil's Edition ___ Using Search Tools ___ Basic Search Strategies ___ Refining Your Search	☐ Pupil's Edition p. 480 ☐ Pupil's Edition p. 480 ☐ Pupil's Edition p. 481
Practice and Apply	
Using Support Materials ___ Using the Web for Research	☐ ✎ mcdougallittell.com
Assess and Close	
Ongoing Assessment Options ___ Assessment Information	☐ 🖥 Teacher's Guide to Assessment and Portfolio Use

---

Homework Assignments

_____
_____
_____
_____
_____
_____
_____
_____
_____
_____

Other Teaching Materials

_____
_____
_____
_____
_____
_____
_____
_____
_____
_____

Lesson 4

Charts and Diagrams

Pages 482–483

Lesson 4 Objectives
To interpret and use graphic aids

Teach	Resources
Warm-Up	
___ Test Preparation	☐ 🏛 Daily Test Prep. p. DT54
Using the Pupil's Edition	
___ Reading and Analyzing Graphic Aids	☐ Pupil's Edition p. 482
___ Types and Purposes of Graphic Aids	☐ Pupil's Edition p. 482

Practice and Apply

Using Support Materials	
___ Reading and Analyzing Graphic Aids	☐ 🖿 Writing and Communication Masters p. 126

Assess and Close

Ongoing Assessment Options	
___ Assessment Information	☐ 🖿 Teacher's Guide to Assessment and Portfolio Use

CHAPTER 26

Homework Assignments

_____
_____
_____
_____
_____
_____
_____
_____
_____
_____

Other Teaching Materials

_____
_____
_____
_____
_____
_____
_____
_____
_____
_____

CHAPTER 26

Lesson 5
Interviews and Surveys

Pages 484–485

Lesson 5 Objectives
To understand how to conduct an interview or survey and to apply this knowledge

Teach

Resources

Warm-Up
___ Test Preparation

☐ 📖 Daily Test Prep. p. DT55

Using the Pupil's Edition
___ Contacting and
Interviewing Experts
___ Using Surveys

☐ Pupil's Edition p. 484

☐ Pupil's Edition p. 484

Assess and Close

Ongoing Assessment Options
___ Assessment Information

☐ 📖 Teacher's Guide to Assessment and Portfolio Use

Homework Assignments

_____
_____
_____
_____
_____
_____
_____
_____
_____
_____

Other Teaching Materials

_____
_____
_____
_____
_____
_____
_____
_____
_____
_____

Preparing for Chapter 27 | Resources

Warm-Up
___ Power Words
___ Write Away

☐ Pupil's Edition p. 488
☐ Pupil's Edition p. 489

Lesson 1 — Separating Facts from Opinions

Pages 490–491

Lesson 1 Objectives
To distinguish between fact and opinion and to apply this knowledge in writing

Teach	Resources

Warm-Up
___ Test Preparation

☐ 🏛 Daily Test Prep. p. DT55

Using the Pupil's Edition
___ Proving Facts
___ Evaluating Opinions

☐ Pupil's Edition p. 490
☐ Pupil's Edition p. 491

Practice and Apply

Using the Pupil's Edition
___ Practice

☐ Pupil's Edition p. 491

Assess and Close

Ongoing Assessment Options
___ Assessment Information

☐ 📖 Teacher's Guide to Assessment and Portfolio Use

CHAPTER 27

Homework Assignments
_____
_____
_____
_____
_____
_____
_____
_____
_____
_____

Other Teaching Materials
_____
_____
_____
_____
_____
_____
_____
_____
_____
_____

Logical Relationships

Lesson 2

Pages 492–494

Lesson 2 Objectives
To identify statements of logical relationships and to use them in writing

Teach | ## Resources

Warm-Up
___ Test Preparation

☐ 🏛 Daily Test Prep. p. DT56

Using the Pupil's Edition
___ Cause and Effect
___ Comparison and Contrast
___ Analogy

☐ Pupil's Edition p. 492
☐ Pupil's Edition p. 493
☐ Pupil's Edition p. 494

Using Support Materials
___ Venn Diagram

☐ 🏛 Critical Thinking Graphic Organizers p. CT7

Practice and Apply

Using Support Materials
___ Practice

☐ Pupil's Edition p. 494

Assess and Close

Ongoing Assessment Options
___ Assessment Information

☐ 📖 Teacher's Guide to Assessment and Portfolio Use

CHAPTER 27

Homework Assignments

Other Teaching Materials

Lesson 3

Interpreting Facts

Pages 495–497

Lesson 3 Objectives
To recognize inferences, conclusions, and generalizations and to make use of them in writing

Teach	Resources

Warm-Up
___ Test Preparation
☐ 📖 Daily Test Prep. p. DT56

Using the Pupil's Edition
___ Making Inferences
___ Drawing Conclusions
___ Forming Generalizations

☐ Pupil's Edition p. 495
☐ Pupil's Edition p. 496
☐ Pupil's Edition p. 497

Practice and Apply

Using the Pupil's Edition
___ Practice A
___ Practice B

☐ Pupil's Edition p. 495
☐ Pupil's Edition p. 496

Assess and Close

Ongoing Assessment Options
___ Assessment Information

☐ 📖 Teacher's Guide to Assessment and Portfolio Use

CHAPTER 27

Homework Assignments
_____
_____
_____
_____
_____
_____
_____
_____
_____
_____
_____
_____

Other Teaching Materials
_____
_____
_____
_____
_____
_____
_____
_____
_____
_____
_____
_____

CHAPTER 27

Lesson 4

Avoiding Errors in Reasoning

Pages 498–499

Lesson 4 Objectives
To recognize instances of the either/or fallacy and of circular reasoning and to correct them in writing

Teach	Resources
Warm-Up	
___ Test Preparation	☐ 🏛 Daily Test Prep. p. DT57
Using the Pupil's Edition	
___ The Either/Or Fallacy	☐ Pupil's Edition p. 498
___ Circular Reasoning	☐ Pupil's Edition p. 499
Using Support Materials	
___ Logical fallacies and Emotional Appeals	☐ 🏛 Writing and Communication Skills p. WC10

Practice and Apply

Using the Pupil's Edition	
___ Practice	☐ Pupil's Edition p. 499

Assess and Close

Ongoing Assessment Options	
___ Assessment Information	☐ 🎞 Teacher's Guide to Assessment and Portfolio Use

---

Homework Assignments

_____
_____
_____
_____
_____
_____
_____
_____
_____

Other Teaching Materials

_____
_____
_____
_____
_____
_____
_____
_____
_____

Misusing Emotional Appeals

Pages 500–501

Lesson 5 Objectives
To recognize misuses of emotional appeals and to correct them in writing

Teach

Resources

Warm-Up
___ Test Preparation

☐ 🏛 Daily Test Prep. p. DT57

Using the Pupil's Edition
___ Name Calling
___ Bandwagon Appeals and Snob Appeals
___ Loaded Language

☐ Pupil's Edition p. 500
☐ Pupil's Edition p. 500

☐ Pupil's Edition p. 501

Using Support Materials
___ Logical Fallacies and Emotional Appeals

☐ 🏛 Writing and Communication Skills p. WC10

Using Technology
___ Analyzing Commercials

☐ 📼 Media Focus: Analyzing and Producing Media, Program 2

Practice and Apply

Using the Pupil's Edition
___ Practice

☐ Pupil's Edition p. 501

Using Support Materials
___ Misusing Emotional Appeals

☐ 📖 Writing and Communication Masters p. 127

Using Technology
___ Media Literacy Activities

☐ ✎ mcdougallittell.com

Assess and Close

Ongoing Assessment Options
___ Assessment Information

☐ 📖 Teacher's Guide to Assessment and Portfolio Use

Homework Assignments
_____
_____
_____
_____
_____
_____
_____
_____
_____

Other Teaching Materials
_____
_____
_____
_____
_____
_____
_____
_____
_____
_____

Preparing for Chapter 28

Resources

Warm-Up
___ Power Words
___ Write Away

☐ Pupil's Edition p. 504
☐ Pupil's Edition p. 505

Lesson 1 Effective Communication

Pages 506–507

Lesson 1 Objectives
To identify and explain kinds of communication and communication barriers

Teach

Resources

Warm-Up
___ Test Preparation

☐ ⚏ Daily Test Prep. p. DT58

Using the Pupil's Edition
___ What is Communication?
___ Communication Barriers

☐ Pupil's Edition p. 506
☐ Pupil's Edition p. 507

Assess and Close

Ongoing Assessment Options
___ Assessment Information

☐ ⚏ Teacher's Guide to Assessment and Portfolio Use

CHAPTER 28

Homework Assignments

_____
_____
_____
_____
_____
_____
_____
_____
_____

Other Teaching Materials

_____
_____
_____
_____
_____
_____
_____
_____
_____

Active Listening

Pages 508–509

Lesson 2 Objectives
To understand listening techniques and to apply this understanding in different listening situations

Teach	Resources

Warm-Up
___ Test Preparation

☐ 📖 Daily Test Prep. p. DT58

Using the Pupil's Edition
___ Listening for Information
___ Critical Listening

☐ Pupil's Edition p. 508
☐ Pupil's Edition p. 509

Assess and Close

Ongoing Assessment Options
___ Assessment Information

☐ 📑 Teacher's Guide to Assessment and Portfolio Use

CHAPTER 28

Homework Assignments

_____
_____
_____
_____
_____
_____
_____
_____
_____
_____

Other Teaching Materials

_____
_____
_____
_____
_____
_____
_____
_____
_____
_____

Lesson 3

Informal Speaking

Pages 510–511

Lesson 3 Objectives
To understand and apply guidelines for informal speaking

Teach	Resources
Warm-Up ___ Test Preparation	☐ 📖 Daily Test Prep. p. DT59
Using the Pupil's Edition ___ Types of Informal Communication	☐ Pupil's Edition p. 510
Assess and Close	
Ongoing Assessment Options ___ Assessment Information	☐ 📋 Teacher's Guide to Assessment and Portfolio Use

CHAPTER 28

Homework Assignments

_____
_____
_____
_____
_____
_____
_____
_____

Other Teaching Materials

_____
_____
_____
_____
_____
_____
_____
_____

Lesson 4

Group Communication

Lesson 4 Objectives
To understand the roles of individuals in groups
To understand and apply guidelines and strategies for discussion

Teach	Resources

Warm-Up
___ Test Preparation

☐ 📖 Daily Test Prep. p. DT59

Using the Pupil's Edition
___ Roles in Groups
___ Group Dynamics

☐ Pupil's Edition p. 512
☐ Pupil's Edition p. 513

Using Support Materials
___ Main Idea Analysis Frame, Rubric for Evaluation

☐ 📖 Critical Thinking Graphic Organizers pp. CT13, 23

Assess and Close

Ongoing Assessment Options
___ Assessment Information

☐ 📖 Teacher's Guide to Assessment and Portfolio Use

CHAPTER 28

Homework Assignments

_____
_____
_____
_____
_____
_____
_____
_____
_____

Other Teaching Materials

_____
_____
_____
_____
_____
_____
_____
_____
_____

Lesson 5

Conducting an Interview

Lesson 5 Objectives
To understand and apply interviewing guidelines and techniques

Teach

Warm-Up
___ Test Preparation

Using the Pupil's Edition
___ Preparation
___ During the Interview
___ Follow-up

Using Support Materials
___ Interviewing Skills

Practice and Apply

Using Support Materials
___ Conducting an Interview

Assess and Close

Ongoing Assessment Options
___ Assessment Information

Resources

☐ 🏛 Daily Test Prep. p. DT60

☐ Pupil's Edition p. 514
☐ Pupil's Edition p. 515
☐ Pupil's Edition p. 515

☐ 🏛 Writing and Communication
　　Skills p. WC11

☐ 📰 Writing and Communication
　　Masters p. 128

☐ 📰 Teacher's Guide to Assess-
　　ment and Portfolio Use

CHAPTER 28

Homework Assignments

_____
_____
_____
_____
_____
_____
_____
_____
_____
_____
_____

Other Teaching Materials

_____
_____
_____
_____
_____
_____
_____
_____
_____
_____
_____

Lesson 6

Formal Speaking

Pages 516–519

Lesson 6 Objectives
To understand and apply guidelines for formal speaking

Teach	Resources
Warm-Up	
___ Test Preparation	☐ 🏛 Daily Test Prep. p. DT60
Using the Pupil's Edition	
___ Recognize Occasion, Purpose, and Audience	☐ Pupil's Edition p. 516
___ Research and Write	☐ Pupil's Edition p. 517
___ Rehearse the Speech	☐ Pupil's Edition p. 518
___ Relax—and Deliver	☐ Pupil's Edition p. 518
___ Evaluating Speakers	☐ Pupil's Edition p. 519
Using Support Materials	
___ Delivering a Speech	☐ 🏛 Writing and Communication Skills p. WC12

Practice and Apply

Using Support Materials	
___ Group Communication	☐ 📖 Writing and Communication Masters p. 129

Assess and Close

Ongoing Assessment Options	
___ Assessment Information	☐ 📖 Teacher's Guide to Assessment and Portfolio Use

Homework Assignments

_____
_____
_____
_____
_____
_____
_____
_____
_____

Other Teaching Materials

_____
_____
_____
_____
_____
_____
_____
_____
_____

CHAPTER 28

Teacher _____ Class _____ Date _____

Preparing for Chapter 29 | Resources

Warm-Up
___ Power Words
___ Write Away

☐ Pupil's Edition p. 522
☐ Pupil's Edition p. 523

 Lesson 1 — # Characteristics of Media

Pages 524–526

Lesson 1 Objectives
To recognize the characteristics of the main types of media: print, broadcast, and the Internet
To compare coverage of a current issue by different media

Teach | Resources

Warm-Up
___ Test Preparation

☐ 🏛 Daily Test Prep. p. DT61

Using the Pupil's Edition
___ Print
___ Broadcast and Film Media
___ Internet

☐ Pupil's Edition p. 524
☐ Pupil's Edition p. 525
☐ Pupil's Edition p. 526

Practice and Apply

Using the Pupil's Edition
___ Practice

☐ Pupil's Edition p. 526

Assess and Close

Ongoing Assessment Options
___ Assessment Information

☐ 🖾 Teacher's Guide to Assessment and Portfolio Use

Homework Assignments
_____
_____
_____
_____
_____
_____
_____
_____
_____

Other Teaching Materials
_____
_____
_____
_____
_____
_____
_____
_____

CHAPTER 29

Copyright © McDougal Littell Inc.

Lesson 2

Influences on the Media

Pages 527–529

Lesson 2 Objectives
To recognize how audiences influence the content of the media
To hypothesize about the reasons for a media decision

Teach	Resources

Warm-Up
___ Test Preparation

☐ 🗒 Daily Test Prep. p. DT61

Using the Pupil's Edition
___ Owners
___ Target Audience
___ Advertisers

☐ Pupil's Edition p. 527
☐ Pupil's Edition p. 527
☐ Pupil's Edition p. 529

Practice and Apply

Using Support Materials
___ Practice A
___ Practice B

☐ Pupil's Edition p. 528
☐ Pupil's Edition p. 529

Assess and Close

Ongoing Assessment Options
___ Assessment Information

☐ 📖 Teacher's Guide to Assessment and Portfolio Use

Homework Assignments

_____
_____
_____
_____
_____
_____
_____
_____
_____
_____
_____

Other Teaching Materials

_____
_____
_____
_____
_____
_____
_____
_____
_____
_____
_____

Messages in the Media

Pages 530–531

Lesson 3 Objectives
To recognize and to identify ways that the media reflect and influence culture

Teach	Resources
Warm-Up ___ Test Preparation	☐ 🖴 Daily Test Prep. p. DT62
Using the Pupil's Edition ___ Reflection of Culture ___ Influence on Culture	☐ Pupil's Edition p. 530 ☐ Pupil's Edition p. 531
Practice and Apply	
Using Support Materials ___ Practice	☐ Pupil's Edition p. 530
Assess and Close	
Ongoing Assessment Options ___ Assessment Information	☐ 🖳 Teacher's Guide to Assessment and Portfolio Use

CHAPTER 29

Homework Assignments

_____
_____
_____
_____
_____
_____
_____
_____
_____
_____
_____

Other Teaching Materials

_____
_____
_____
_____
_____
_____
_____
_____
_____
_____
_____

Lesson 4

Evaluating Media

Pages 532–535

Lesson 4 Objectives
To recognize and apply strategies for analyzing the core purpose of media messages

To evaluate the content and presentation of media

Teach | Resources

Warm-Up
___ Test Preparation

☐ 🏛 Daily Test Prep. p. DT62

Using the Pupil's Edition
___ Analyzing Purpose in Media
___ Evaluating Content
___ Evaluating Presentation

☐ Pupil's Edition p. 532

☐ Pupil's Edition p. 533
☐ Pupil's Edition p. 534

Using Technology
___ Analyzing Film, Analyzing TV News

☐ 📼 Media Focus: Analyzing and Producing Media, Programs 1, 3

Practice and Apply

Using Support Materials
___ Practice A
___ Practice B

☐ Pupil's Edition p. 532
☐ Pupil's Edition p. 535

Using Technology
___ Media Literacy Activities

☐ 💬 mcdougallittell.com

Assess and Close

Ongoing Assessment Options
___ Assessment Information

☐ 🖼 Teacher's Guide to Assessment and Portfolio Use

Homework Assignments
_____
_____
_____
_____
_____
_____
_____
_____

Other Teaching Materials
_____
_____
_____
_____
_____
_____
_____
_____

CHAPTER 29

Preparing for Chapter 30

Resources

Warm-Up
___ Power Words
___ Write Away

☐ Pupil's Edition p. 538
☐ Pupil's Edition p. 539

Lesson 1 # Using Media

Pages 540–541

Lesson 1 Objectives

To recognize different types of media and to choose a medium suitable for a particular audience, message, and purpose

Teach

Resources

Warm-Up
___ Test Preparation

☐ 📖 Daily Test Prep. p. DT63

Using the Pupil's Edition
___ Media Options
___ Targeting Your Audience
___ Choosing a Medium

☐ Pupil's Edition p. 540
☐ Pupil's Edition p. 540
☐ Pupil's Edition p. 541

Practice and Apply

Using Support Materials
___ Media Literacy Activities

☐ 🔗 mcdougallittell.com

Assess and Close

Ongoing Assessment Options
___ Assessment Information

☐ 🎞 Teacher's Guide to Assessment and Portfolio Use

Homework Assignments

Other Teaching Materials

CHAPTER 30

Lesson 2 · Creating Videos

Pages 542–545

Lesson 2 Objectives
To understand the steps involved in planning and creating a video; to follow these steps to produce a video

Teach	Resources

Warm-Up
___ Test Preparation

☐ 🏛 Daily Test Prep. p. DT63

Using the Pupil's Edition
___ Pre-Production
___ Production
___ Post-Production
___ Evaluating and Revising

☐ Pupil's Edition p. 542
☐ Pupil's Edition p. 543
☐ Pupil's Edition p. 545
☐ Pupil's Edition p. 545

Using Technology
___ Creating Student Videos

☐ 📼 Media Focus: Analyzing and Producing Media, Programs 4

Practice and Apply

Using Technology
___ Media Literacy Activities

☐ 🌐 mcdougallittell.com

Assess and Close

Ongoing Assessment Options
___ Assessment Information

☐ 📘 Teacher's Guide to Assessment and Portfolio Use

Homework Assignments

_____
_____
_____
_____
_____
_____
_____
_____
_____
_____

Other Teaching Materials

_____
_____
_____
_____
_____
_____
_____
_____
_____
_____

CHAPTER 30

Lesson 3 Planning Multimedia Presentations

Pages 546–547

Lesson 3 Objectives
To understand the steps involved in planning and creating a multimedia presentation; to follow these steps to create a multimedia presentation

Teach	Resources
Warm-Up	
___ Test Preparation	☐ 🏛 Daily Test Prep. p. DT64
Using the Pupil's Edition	
___ Planning and Organizing	☐ Pupil's Edition p. 546
___ Developing the Presentation	☐ Pupil's Edition p. 547
___ Evaluating and Revising	☐ Pupil's Edition p. 547
Using Support Materials	
___ Sequence Chain	☐ 🏛 Critical Thinking Graphic Organizers p. CT9
Using Technology	
___ Creating Multimedia Projects	☐ 📼 Media Focus: Analyzing and Producing Media, Programs 5

Practice and Apply

Using Technology	
___ Media Literacy Activities	☐ 🔎 mcdougallittell.com

Assess and Close

Ongoing Assessment Options	
___ Assessment Information	☐ 🖥 Teacher's Guide to Assessment and Portfolio Use

Homework Assignments

_____
_____
_____
_____
_____
_____
_____

Other Teaching Materials

_____
_____
_____
_____
_____
_____
_____

CHA

Lesson 4

Creating a Web Site

Pages 548–549

Lesson 4 Objectives
To understand the steps involved in planning and developing a Web site; to follow these steps to create a Web site

Teach

Warm-Up
___ Test Preparation

Using the Pupil's Edition
___ Planning the Site
___ Developing the Web Site
___ Evaluating and Revising

Assess and Close

Ongoing Assessment Options
___ Assessment Information

Resources

☐ 📖 Daily Test Prep. p. DT64

☐ Pupil's Edition p. 548
☐ Pupil's Edition p. 549
☐ Pupil's Edition p. 549

☐ 🖼 Teacher's Guide to Assessment and Portfolio Use

Homework Assignments

_____
_____
_____
_____
_____
_____
_____
_____
_____
_____

Other Teaching Materials

_____
_____
_____
_____
_____
_____
_____
_____
_____
_____

CHAPTER 30

Preparing for Chapter 31 | Resources

Warm-Up
___ Power Words
___ Write Away

☐ Pupil's Edition p. 552
☐ Pupil's Edition p. 553

(Lesson 1) Using Vocabulary Strategies   *Page 554*

Lesson 1 Objectives
To recognize and use different strategies to determine the meanings of unfamiliar words

Teach	Resources
Warm-Up	
___ Test Preparation	☐ 🏛 Daily Test Prep. p. DT65
Using the Pupil's Edition	
___ Here's the Idea	☐ Pupil's Edition p. 554

Practice and Apply

Using Technology	
___ Vocabulary Practice Flipcards	☐ 🖱 mcdougallittell.com

Assess and Close

Ongoing Assessment Options	
___ Assessment Information	☐ 📖 Teacher's Guide to Assessment and Portfolio Use

Homework Assignments

_____
_____
_____
_____
_____
_____
_____
_____
_____
_____
_____

Other Teaching Materials

_____
_____
_____
_____
_____
_____
_____
_____
_____
_____
_____

CHAPTER 31

Lesson 2

Understanding Word Parts

Pages 555–557

Lesson 2 Objectives
To identify word parts and to analyze them to determine the meanings of unfamiliar words

Teach	Resources
Warm-Up ___ Test Preparation	☐ 🏛 Daily Test Prep. p. DT65
Using the Pupil's Edition ___ Base Words and Roots ___ Prefixes ___ Suffixes	☐ Pupil's Edition p. 555 ☐ Pupil's Edition p. 556 ☐ Pupil's Edition p. 557
Using Support Materials ___ Roots, Prefixes, Suffixes, Word Families	☐ 🏛 Vocabulary pp. VO4–7

Practice and Apply

Using the Pupil's Edition ___ Practice	☐ Pupil's Edition p. 557
Using Support Materials ___ Analyzing Word Parts	☐ 🖿 Writing and Communication Masters p. 130
Using Technology ___ Vocabulary Flipcards	☐ 🖱 mcdougallittell.com

Assess and Close

Ongoing Assessment Options ___ Assessment Information	☐ 🖿 Teacher's Guide to Assess- ment and Portfolio Use

Homework Assignments
_____
_____
_____
_____
_____
_____
_____

Other Teaching Materials
_____
_____
_____
_____
_____
_____
_____
_____

CHAPTER 31

Lesson 3 · Using Context Clues

Pages 558–559

Lesson 3 Objectives
To identify and use context clues to determine the meanings of unfamiliar words

Teach	Resources

Warm-Up

___ Test Preparation
☐ 🏛 Daily Test Prep. p. DT66

Using the Pupil's Edition

___ Definition and
Restatement Clues ☐ Pupil's Edition p. 558

___ Example Clues ☐ Pupil's Edition p. 558

___ Contrast Clues ☐ Pupil's Edition p. 559

___ General Context Clues ☐ Pupil's Edition p. 559

Using Support Materials

___ Context Clues ☐ 🏛 Vocabulary pp. VO1–3

Practice and Apply

Using the Pupil's Edition

___ Practice ☐ Pupil's Edition p. 559

Using Support Materials

___ Using Context Clues ☐ 📰 Writing and Communication Masters p. 131

Using Technology

___ Vocabulary Flipcards ☐ 🖉 mcdougallittell.com

Assess and Close

Ongoing Assessment Options

___ Assessment Information ☐ 📰 Teacher's Guide to Assessment and Portfolio Use

Homework Assignments

_____
_____
_____
_____
_____
_____
_____
_____

Other Teaching Materials

_____
_____
_____
_____
_____
_____
_____
_____

CHAPTER 31

Lesson 4

Using Vocabulary Reference Books

Pages 560–561

Lesson 4 Objectives
To identify and use various reference resources to expand vocabulary

Teach	Resources
Warm-Up ___ Test Preparation	☐ 🏛 Daily Test Prep. p. DT66
Using the Pupil's Edition ___ Dictionaries ___ Thesauruses and Other Vocabulary References	☐ Pupil's Edition p. 560 ☐ Pupil's Edition p. 561
Practice and Apply	
Using the Pupil's Edition ___ Practice	☐ Pupil's Edition p. 561
Using Technology ___ Vocabulary Flipcards	☐ 🖱 mcdougallittell.com
Assess and Close	
Ongoing Assessment Options ___ Assessment Information	☐ 📖 Teacher's Guide to Assessment and Portfolio Use

Homework Assignments

_____
_____
_____
_____
_____
_____
_____
_____
_____
_____

Other Teaching Materials

_____
_____
_____
_____
_____
_____
_____
_____
_____
_____

CHAPTER 31

Exploring Shades of Meaning

Pages 562–563

Lesson 5 Objectives
To understand the shades of meaning among similar words and to use words more precisely in speaking and writing

Teach	Resources
Warm-Up	
___ Test Preparation	☐ 📖 Daily Test Prep. p. DT67
Using the Pupil's Edition	
___ Synonyms	☐ Pupil's Edition p. 562
___ Denotation and Connotation	☐ Pupil's Edition p. 562
___ Antonyms	☐ Pupil's Edition p. 563
Using Support Materials	
___ Multiple Meanings	☐ 📖 Vocabulary p. VO8

Practice and Apply

Using the Pupil's Edition	
___ Practice	☐ Pupil's Edition p. 563
Using Technology	
___ Vocabulary Flipcards	☐ 🖱 mcdougallittell.com

Assess and Close

Ongoing Assessment Options	
___ Assessment Information	☐ 📖 Teacher's Guide to Assessment and Portfolio Use

---

Homework Assignments

_____
_____
_____
_____
_____
_____
_____
_____
_____
_____

Other Teaching Materials

_____
_____
_____
_____
_____
_____
_____
_____
_____
_____

Preparing for Chapter 32

Resources

Warm-Up
___ Power Words
___ Write Away

☐ Pupil's Edition p. 566
☐ Pupil's Edition p. 567

Lesson 1 — Studying in the Content Areas

Pages 568–570

Lesson 1 Objectives
To recognize and apply active reading strategies in studying mathematics, history, and science

Teach

Resources

Warm-Up
___ Test Preparation

☐ 🏛 Daily Test Prep. p. DT67

Using the Pupil's Edition
___ Active Reading Strategies
___ Reading and Studying Mathematics
___ Reading and Studying History
___ Reading and Studying Science

☐ Pupil's Edition p. 568
☐ Pupil's Edition p. 568
☐ Pupil's Edition p. 569
☐ Pupil's Edition p. 570

Using Support Materials
___ Venn Diagram, Main Idea Analysis Frame, Cause-and-Effect Chart

☐ 🏛 Critical Thinking Graphic Organizers pp. CT7, 13, 15

Practice and Apply

Using Support Materials
___ Active Reading Strategies

☐ 🖥 Writing and Communication Masters p. 132

Using Technology
___ Test Practice

☐ 🖱 mcdougallittell.com

Assess and Close

Ongoing Assessment Options
___ Assessment Information

☐ 🖥 Teacher's Guide to Assessment and Portfolio Use

Homework Assignments
_____
_____
_____
_____
_____
_____
_____
_____
_____
_____
_____
_____

Other Teaching Materials
_____
_____
_____
_____
_____
_____
_____
_____
_____
_____
_____
_____

CHAPTER 32

Teacher _____ Class _____ Date _____

Lesson 2

Test Preparation

Pages 571–572

Lesson 2 Objectives
To recognize and apply strategies for taking objective tests

Teach	**Resources**
Warm-Up	
___ Test Preparation	☐ 📖 Daily Test Prep. p. DT68
Using the Pupil's Edition	
___ Objective Tests	☐ Pupil's Edition p. 571
Practice and Apply	
Using Support Materials	
___ Answering Objective Test Questions	☐ 📄 Writing and Communication Masters p. 133
Using Technology	
___ Test Practice	☐ 🖱 mcdougallittell.com
Assess and Close	
Ongoing Assessment Options	
___ Assessment Information	☐ 📄 Teacher's Guide to Assessment and Portfolio Use

Homework Assignments
_____
_____
_____
_____
_____
_____
_____
_____
_____
_____
_____
_____

Other Teaching Materials
_____
_____
_____
_____
_____
_____
_____
_____
_____
_____
_____
_____

Lesson 3

Standardized Testing: Vocabulary

Pages 573–575

Lesson 3 Objectives
To recognize and apply strategies for taking standardized vocabulary tests

Teach	Resources
Warm-Up ___ Test Preparation	☐ 📖 Daily Test Prep. p. DT68
Using the Pupil's Edition ___ Synonyms and Antonyms ___ Analogies	☐ Pupil's Edition p. 573 ☐ Pupil's Edition p. 574

Practice and Apply

Using the Pupil's Edition ___ Practice A ___ Practice A	☐ Pupil's Edition p. 573 ☐ Pupil's Edition p. 575
Using Technology ___ Test Practice	☐ 🖥 mcdougallittell.com

Assess and Close

Ongoing Assessment Options ___ Assessment Information	☐ 📷 Teacher's Guide to Assessment and Portfolio Use

Homework Assignments

_____
_____
_____
_____
_____
_____
_____
_____
_____
_____
_____

Other Teaching Materials

_____
_____
_____
_____
_____
_____
_____
_____
_____
_____
_____

CHAPTER 32

Lesson 4

Standardized Testing: Reading

Pages 576–577

Lesson 4 Objectives
To recognize and apply strategies for taking standardized reading comprehension tests

Teach	Resources
Warm-Up	
___ Test Preparation	☐ 📖 Daily Test Prep. p. DT69
Using the Pupil's Edition	
___ Reading Comprehension	☐ Pupil's Edition p. 576
Practice and Apply	
Using the Pupil's Edition	
___ Practice	☐ Pupil's Edition p. 577
Using Technology	
___ Test Practice	☐ 🖱 mcdougallittell.com
Assess and Close	
Ongoing Assessment Options	
___ Assessment Information	☐ 📓 Teacher's Guide to Assessment and Portfolio Use

Homework Assignments	Other Teaching Materials
_____	_____
_____	_____
_____	_____
_____	_____
_____	_____
_____	_____
_____	_____
_____	_____
_____	_____
_____	_____
_____	_____
_____	_____

CHAPTER 32

Lesson 5

Answering Essay Questions

Lesson 5 Objectives
To recognize and apply strategies for answering essay questions

Teach

Resources

Warm-Up
___ Test Preparation

☐ 🏛 Daily Test Prep. p. DT69

Using the Pupil's Edition
___ Analyzing the Prompt
___ Planning and Writing
Your Answer
___ Evaluating Your Work

☐ Pupil's Edition p. 578
☐ Pupil's Edition p. 579

☐ Pupil's Edition p. 579

Practice and Apply

Using Support Materials
___ Answering Essay
Questions

☐ 📖 Writing and Communication
Masters p. 134

Using Technology
___ Test Practice

☐ 🖱 mcdougallittell.com

Assess and Close

Ongoing Assessment Options
___ Assessment Information

☐ 📖 Teacher's Guide to Assessment and Portfolio Use

Homework Assignments

_____
_____
_____
_____
_____
_____
_____
_____
_____
_____
_____
_____

Other Teaching Materials

_____
_____
_____
_____
_____
_____
_____
_____
_____
_____
_____
_____

CHAPTER 32